M000164236

The
Sultan's Organ

London to Constantinople in 1599 and adventures on the way

the diary of

THOMAS DALLAM

put into modern English by

JOHN MOLE

First published by Fortune in 2012

www.fortunebooks.org

This translation copyright © 2012 John Mole

The right of John Mole to be identified as author of this work
has been asserted in accordance with the Copyright, Designs and
Patents Act 1988.

ISBN:978-0-9557569-2-4

Cover by Olivia Mole

CONTENTS

1 INTRODUCTION

In 1598 merchants of the City of London paid for a Present to be given by Queen Elizabeth to Sultan Mehmet III of Turkey. The merchants wanted trading concessions. The Queen wanted the Sultan's fleet to attack Spain. The Present was a chiming clock with jewel-encrusted moving figures combined with an automatic organ, which could play tunes on its own for six hours. It could also be played by hand. It was in a carved and painted and gilded cabinet about sixteen feet high, six feet wide and five feet deep.

The Present was dismantled and loaded onto a merchant ship early in 1599. It took six months to get from London to Constantinople. With it went four craftsmen. They were Thomas Dallam the organ builder,

John Harvey the engineer, Michael Watson the carpenter and Rowland Buckett the painter. Dallam was about twenty four years old.

They encountered storms, pirates, exotic animals, foreign food, good wine, volcanoes, Moors, Turks, Greeks, Jews, beautiful women, barbarous men, kings and pashas, armies on the march, brigands, janissaries, eunuchs, slaves, dwarves and finally the most powerful man in the world, the Great Turk himself.

For those of us who have an insular and nationalistic vision of Elizabethan England formed by Shakespeare, school history, film and TV, Dallam's diary opens up the wider world that Elizabethans lived in. Many English people of all social classes made their homes in the Mediterranean. Two Muslim Turkish interpreters worked with Dallam. One was born in Lancashire and the other in Cornwall.

We most often see Elizabethan England through the eyes of the aristocratic and wealthy. Thomas Dallam gives us the point of view of the skilled working man. He has not been to grammar school or university so does not distort the scenery with classical or biblical references and when he tries usually gets it wrong. He writes fluently and colloquially in an English not deformed by classical education. He writes what he sees and experiences as plainly as he can. Above all he has an open mind towards foreigners. His attitude to Turks and Muslims is conditioned by the racism and paranoia of his age but when he actually meets them he interacts without prejudice.

My purpose is to let Dallam describe his experiences without the impediments of spelling, vocabulary and grammar peculiar to Elizabethan English and without the distraction of footnotes and references. I have resisted the temptation to edit the boring or repetitive bits as they give a rhythm to the journey and a setting for the fascinating passages. I have translated the place names into their modern equivalents so you can follow the journey on an atlas or Google.

The Sultan was the most powerful ruler in the world. No foreigner, unless they were a concubine or a eunuch, ever came closer to him than Thomas Dallam. He played for the Sultan, touched him, received gold from his pocket. He is the first foreigner to peek inside the Sultan's harem and live to write about it. He is the first to describe an overland journey in Greece. For these alone his diary is worth reading. But mainly it is because he tells a great story.

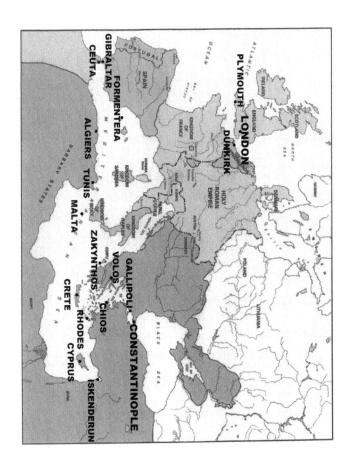

2 A CURIOUS PRESENT

A great and curious present is going to the Grand Turk,
which will scandalize other nations.
John Chamberlain to Dudley Carleton, 31 January 1599

ON THE HOUR...

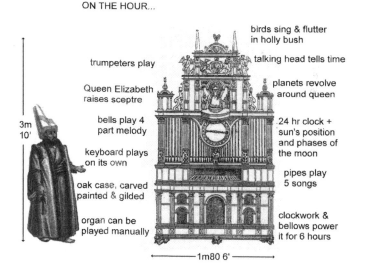

trumpeters play

Queen Elizabeth
raises sceptre

3m
10'

bells play 4
part melody

keyboard plays
on its own

oak case, carved
painted & gilded

organ can be
played manually

birds sing & flutter
in holly bush

talking head tells time

planets revolve
around queen

24 hr clock +
sun's position
and phases of
the moon

pipes play
5 songs

clockwork &
bellows power
it for 6 hours

1m80 6'

3 THE JOURNEY

DEPARTURE

February 1599

With no friends to advise me, these were my last-minute purchases for the journey to Turkey: a suit of sackcloth to wear at sea; a second wool suit; two flannel waistcoats; a hat; a sword; a chest; nine shirts; a dozen and a half collars; a dozen handkerchiefs; one pair of garters; two dozen laces; two pairs of stockings; one pair of linen breeches; a pair of pumps and a pair of slippers; three pairs of shoes; a sword belt and loops; a gown; a little harpsichord; a pair of thick breeches; two hat bands; a box of drinking glasses; Rosa Solis liqueur and preserved fruit; oil and vinegar; prunes; raisins; cloves, mace, and pepper; two pounds of sugar; nutmegs; gloves; knives; 30lbs of tin in bars; a gross of spoons; oatmeal. *(The tin was for making and mending organ pipes.)*

February 9th

The ship in which I was to sail to Constantinople was moored at Gravesend. I left London in a rowing boat with my chest and provisions on Friday the 9th of February 1599. When I got to Gravesend, I went on board our ship, the Hector, with my chest, my bedding and the little harpsichord, which the merchants allowed me to bring, so I could practice on the way. I had no other luggage except for a gross of tin spoons, which cost me nine shillings, and thirty pounds of tin in bars, which cost me eighteen shillings. *(The Hector, 300 tons, 100 crew Privately owned but with 27 guns as powerful as a warship of the Queen's navy.)*

The ship was not at all ready and none of the passenger cabins was made up so I had to go into town to find board and lodging until the afternoon of the 13th when we weighed anchor. We sailed as far as Deal Castle, where we anchored, as there was not enough wind to take us past Dover. We waited four days.

We went ashore to Deal and Sandwich to enjoy ourselves. When the wind came up in the night, a few of us passengers and sailors were in Deal. Some of us had a lot to drink, especially one of our five trumpeters, who locked the door of his bedroom. When the man from the ship came to fetch us, he stood under his window and called up. The trumpeter came to the window and shouted abuse at him, so we all went back to the ship and left the drunkard behind.

STORM

The wind was fair and we sailed past Dover and along the Channel. But when we had gone about a hundred and twenty miles the wind changed and a great storm blew up. It lasted forty eight hours. In the night we not only lost our pinnace, the Lanneret, which was due to sail with us to the Gulf of Venice, but we ourselves were lost. The fog was so thick we could see nothing. When it began to clear we found ourselves close to the Casquet Rocks between England and Ireland, a very dangerous place. The crew struggled to get into the open sea again but the storm continued and the fog got worse. The next day we had no idea where we were, and still under sail in the thick fog. Suddenly we saw waves breaking on great rocks. We were so close to the shore we had no time to go about and save ourselves from shipwreck. But it pleased Almighty God to keep us from harm. We were just in front of Dartmouth harbour with its great rocks on either side of the entrance and we sailed in, very relieved.

We stayed there four days. Meanwhile our captain and the merchants sent messengers to all the harbour towns along the coast to enquire about our pinnace, the Lanneret. In the end word arrived that after the storm she was chased by three or four Dunkirk privateers. The topmast was broken in the storm and she avoided capture by coming ashore at Falmouth. There she got a new topmast and sent word by the messenger that she would meet us in Plymouth Sound. We weighed anchor and set sail. At Plymouth we fired a gun to summon the pinnace but the wind changed and we had to drop anchor in the Cattewater. We met up with the pinnace but we waited seven days for a wind. *(A pinnace is a small vessel used by a larger ship to ferry supplies or messages)*

PIRATES

March 16th

The weather was very cold but the wind blew fair. We were under sail in Plymouth Sound, when a boat loaded with salt came in. As soon as they reached the shore and heard the name of our ship, they blew a trumpet to ask for a meeting. We struck sail and two of their crew came aboard. They advised our captain not to set sail without a convoy of other vessels. They had been at sea in a man-of-war from Plymouth called the Plough and were captured by seven Dunkirk pirate ships. They were questioned about the whereabouts of the Hector and whether she had set out on her voyage, but they insisted that they had never heard of such a ship. Some of the men were killed on the spot to strike fear into the others. They did not know what happened to the rest. The Dunkirkers took their ship and gave six of them the boat to take them home. Our captain heard these men out and told them he would not wait so much as an hour for more of a convoy than God had already sent him. This amounted to our pinnace and two ships heading for Newfoundland, which caught us up for their own safety. *(Dunkirk and other Flemish ports belonged to Spain which was at war with England. Piracy was political as well as mercenary)*

The wind was fair and our ship made such speed that we could lend the pinnace our mainsail. Yet the next morning she was very far behind. At about 8 o'clock in the morning the lookout in the topmast saw three sails on our port bow. Shortly afterwards he saw four more on the same course. These were the seven ships we had been warned about. We made ready. The gunners prepared their artillery, the waist cloths were put up, and every man had his bandoleer and musket. *(Waist cloths were fabric screens to conceal the crew in battle or as ornamentation.)* We had the wind and need not have spoken with them, but our captain thought it better not to appear afraid or cowardly in case the wind suddenly turned and our running away encouraged them to attack us. He ordered the bosun to head towards them, which he did with a will. When we came close enough to make out their lead ship and its second coming boldly towards us, our captain ordered the bosun to show them a broadside, for our mainsail was so big they could not see the strength of our ship. He said

"Perhaps they may take our ship to be one of the Queen's. If we do happen to hail them or they us, tell them our ship is called the Seven Stars, for the Queen doesn't have one yet with that name." But as soon as they saw the broadside they thought we were indeed one of the Queen's ships and went about to run away.

We gave chase and almost lost sight of our pinnace and the other ships in our convoy. The pirates made all the sail they could and yet within half an hour we were in range of them. Our captain ordered the master gunner to fire a bow gun at the lead ship but not to hit her. The master gunner gave her a shot across the bows but they neither struck sail nor showed a flag. They made off with all the sail they had, from drabblers to topgallants, *(extra sails below and above the mainsail)* but without effect for we came nearer and nearer to them. Our captain ordered the gunner to shoot through the lead ship's mainsail, which he did very close to the drabbler. Then he shot the tops of the mainmasts of the lead ship, the second and the third. They were to windward of us, but although we came up alongside, nobody showed himself. Then the bosun of our ship stood on the forecastle with his sword drawn and ordered them to come to our lee side. They did so very reluctantly. We were by now very close to the coast of Spain, or France, so the bosun tacked again to get back on our right course. All seven ships followed us. Then our captain called their commander, ordering him to lower a boat and come aboard us, or he would sink them. After calling the second time a man who by his speech was a Dutchman answered 'we will, we will,' but it was a long time before their boat appeared. At last they launched their boat with the captain and four sailors to row it. They went aboard their second ship and stayed half an hour. Then the three captains came on board our ship. All this time we were keeping our course and all seven of them dared do nothing but follow us.

When the three captains came aboard, we noticed that one of them carried under his arm a long money bag, full of something. They went with our captain into his cabin and talked for a good while. In the meantime the sailors who had brought the captains on board stood on our hatches. Our sailors were looking them over and one of our men said

"I'm sure I know that fellow. He's an Englishman." The other man swore that he was no Englishman, yet he spoke as good English as any of us.

Then one of our mates, the purser and bosun took their boat with four of our own sailors and went on board three or four of their ships. In the meantime our captain finished his discussion with the three captains and came out of his cabin, strode onto the spar deck and summoned our crew. He read out a letter which looked as if it had been recently written. It was made out like a pass from the King of France for wine that the captains said their ships were carrying. But while he was reading the letter our mate, purser and bosun came back from the ships saying they were men of war laden with nothing but soldiers, muskets, swords and daggers, shields and bucklers, and intended only to capture us. But our captain, who had already taken his bribe in the cabin, was very angry with his mate and the purser for saying so and said he had a letter to the contrary. He released the captains and let the ships go, which very much grieved the crew and the rest of us.

If he had done what he could have done, which was to bring these seven ships as a prize to England, it would have been the greatest service that an English merchant ship had ever performed and would have done us great credit. By the time we came back from Turkey it was well known that between the time they escaped from us and the time we arrived home, those seven ships had taken and robbed three score of English and other country's ships between London and Newcastle. *(Perhaps reflecting his opinion of the captain, Dallam never mentions him by name, which was Richard Parsons)*

GIBRALTAR

March 20th

With a fair wind we passed the North Cape and entered the Bay of Portugal.

March 23rd

We rounded the South Cape and were becalmed for a time.

March 24th

A great school of porpoises leaped and swam around us, a marvellous sight.

March 25th

We saw gigantic fish or whales which spouted water up into the air, like smoke out of a chimney. Sometimes we saw a large part of their bodies out of the water. Still no wind.

March 27th

With a fair wind that blew up strong about 11 or 12 o'clock we entered the Strait of Gibraltar, in defiance of our enemies. *(Spain, at war with England, held the Strait)* At the entrance it is only twelve miles at the most from shore to shore. It looked to me no more than three miles because the land is very high on both sides, Spain on the left and North Africa on the right. On the Spanish side we saw a very fine town close to the sea called Tarifa. On the North African side there is an enormous mountain of rock called Ape Hill. Thirty miles further, on the Spanish side, there is a well fortified town called Gibraltar. Many of the King of Spain's galleys and men of war lie at anchor there to defend the Strait. On the east side of the town is a great mountain on which a large part of the town is built. The mountain rises steeply on both sides and on the east side so vertically that it cannot be climbed. At the end is a solid bulwark to protect the town.

When we set out from Plymouth on the 6th of March the weather was very cold with not a trace of green on the trees or hedges. On the 27th at the entrance to the Strait the weather was very hot, the fields on either side very green and the trees all in leaf. I was amazed at the change in just eleven days.

Directly opposite Gibraltar on the North African side there is a fine looking town called Ceuta. It is surrounded by walls and pleasant fields with good soil. Although there are huge mountains and jagged rocks on both sides, a little to the east of the town there is a solid fort and the same on the west side. Although it is in North Africa, the town belongs to the King of Spain.

A little further along the Spanish coast is the town of Marbella but I could not see much of it because of the fog. The next town is Malaga and then Salobrenia, which is one hundred and sixty miles east of Gibraltar.

March 28th

We carried on along the coast of Spain. We could see tall mountains permanently capped with snow ,while down in the valleys it is very hot.

March 29th

We sailed along the coast of Africa.

ALGIERS

March 30th

We came into a harbour in North Africa called Algiers. *(Noted for trade, piracy and slavery. The King owed allegiance to the Sultan)* From the sea the town looked very beautiful. It lies close to the water on a very steep hill. In its proportions the town is like a topsail. It is well fortified with a double wall and a ditch. The houses are built of stone and cement. Most of the houses have flat roofs skilfully laid with plaster of Paris. From the top of one house you can get over the roofs to most parts of the town. Some of the streets are very narrow and hard going because the town is built on rocks. Above the town on top of the hill is a castle which commands the roadstead, which is the stretch of sea in front of the town. Almost a mile inland is another castle with a small garrison. I was told it is only to guard the springs which feed the fountains in the town, for the Turks drink nothing but water. They say that a horse and rider can go from the castle to the town through a tunnel underground.

With three or four others I went a mile inland where we saw another castle which we thought was for the same purpose. We went so far inland at the request of Mr Chancy, who was our ship's doctor and wanted to gather herbs and roots. This was the last day of March and it was amazing how forward spring was. Trees and hedges were in leaf; corn, wheat and barley had sprouted; young oranges and lemons were on the trees. Coming back into town we met Moors and other people driving donkeys loaded with green beans to be sold in the market. As they went along the street they called out 'balock, balock' that is to say 'beware' or 'watch out'. We saw some Moors come riding in completely naked but for a little cloth like a child's apron. Some carried spears, others bows and arrows. *(Moors was a general term for natives of North Africa, usually applied to people of Berber extraction.)*

There are also many Jews living there but the majority are Turks. The town, or city I should say, is full of people for it is an important trading centre. They have two market days a week. Large numbers of people come out of the mountains and other parts of the country bringing in loads of corn and all sorts of fruit, as well as wild and domestic fowl. There is a lot of partridge and quail which are very cheap, a partridge for less than a penny and three quails for the same price. There are also lots of hens and chickens. They are artificially hatched in ovens or hot houses without the assistance of a hen. At this moment I cannot describe exactly how it is done but I will do so later, God willing. They also have large herds of camels, donkeys big and small, oxen, horses and riding camels.

Many Turks are converted Christians of all nationalities. Most of them are Spaniards, Italians and men from adjoining countries, who, when they are captured, are forced to convert or else live in slavery and misery. Over time these renegade Christians become barbaric and wicked, taking pleasure in all kinds of nefarious activities. What they most enjoy is prowling about the coasts of other countries, with all the skill and trickery they can muster, to betray Christians and sell them into slavery to the Moors and other merchants of North Africa.

There are many hot-houses or baths which they call bagnios, and cook shops that do very good meat. The day after we anchored in the roadstead, the king summoned our captain to bring the Present he was taking to the Sultan. The captain went and told him that the Present was not only big and heavy but also very complicated and would take a long time to assemble for viewing. The king did not believe him but kept him prisoner and sent for me and my assistant. When we came before him and were interrogated he found we told the same story. Only then did he release our captain. The king then sent the captain a present of two bulls and three sheep, which were very scrawny, since they think that the poorest things they have are too good for Christians. In general they are all very grasping and use all their ingenuity to get as much as they can from Christians, legitimately or not.

In the street Turkish and Moorish women cover their faces. They believe the women have no souls, so it is said. I think it would be good for them if they did not, for they never go to church or other prayers, like the men. The men are very religious in their own way and have very beautiful churches called mosques.

SICILY

April 4th

We left Algiers and sailed along the coast of Africa. Eighty miles from Algiers there is a fine-looking town called Dalis but we kept our distance. We also passed a little town called Annaba or Hippo, under a tall mountain rising to a peak like a sugar-loaf. Some of our sailors said St Augustine once kept a school or a clergy-house there. It is a hundred and twenty miles from Algiers.

April 7th

The day before Easter we saw amazing lightning. The sky was opened by a streak of fire like a very hot iron from a blacksmith's forge. Sometimes it looked like a wriggling worm, another time a horseshoe, and again like a leg or a foot. The thunder claps were deafening.

April 8th

We passed a huge mountain which is in fact an island close to the shore. It is called Zembra. On the coast opposite was once the city of Carthage. About twenty miles further on we saw Cape Bon. On the west side is a large town called Tunis where a number of Turkish galleys are moored.

April 14th

We sailed close to the shore of the famous island of Sicily. It is said to be two hundred and forty miles long. A very fertile and pleasant land, it yields a great deal of corn and all kinds of fruit. On the east side are always moored at least nine galleys and on the west side ten or more. At the eastern end of Sicily is a very high mountain which they call Montabell but whose proper name is Etna. In the daytime we could see the top covered in snow and at night bursts of flame coming from what we thought was the centre of the mountain. This great island is ruled by the King of Spain. We passed it on the left side and then on the right saw Malta, likewise under the King of Spain. It is now held by the Knights of Rhodes so the Turks cannot pass that way.

April 15th

Before we reached Malta, we gave chase to a ship. When her captain saw from our flag what we were and that he could not resist us, he launched his boat and came aboard us. He brought a present of various goods, Turkish carpets, quilts of light blue silk, and two or three pieces of salt fish seven or eight foot long and a foot wide. It looked a strange fish to us. We never tasted it, for after their captain spoke privately with ours he was allowed to leave and to take all his presents with him. It grieved our sailors because some of our officers boarded the other ship while he was talking with our captain and discovered in the purser's books that they had ten thousand dollars worth of Spanish goods on board. Having received a secret bribe our captain told us that the ship came from

Chios where Mr. William Aldridge was consul, along with other empty excuses, and so he would not take anything. So the ship went away and we passed by Malta.

April 17th

We gave chase to a ship from Marseilles and boarded her but got little or nothing from her. Then we crossed the Ionian Sea.

April 19th

We made landfall in Greece.

ZAKYNTHOS

April 20th

We passed Argostoli on our left hand. It has two towns and an exceptionally good harbour. Nearby is the island of Zakynthos. *(Dallam calls it Zante, the Italian name still used by many British.)* We anchored before the main town which is also called Zakynthos and has a good harbour. The town is close to the sea and is about a mile long. Behind it on a very high and steep hill is a castle where the governor lives. He is called the Providore. Within the castle walls are various other residents and many houses. The Providore holds court twice a week to hear cases brought by Greeks as well as Venetians and Italians. The Duke of Venice holds the island from the Sultan and pays tribute for it. The majority of the population is Greek. They work hard planting and pruning currant gardens, olive groves and vineyards. They grow very little corn but most of our currants and the best oil comes from there. They also have good wine. They import bread, beef, goats, sheep, pigs and chickens from Chlemoutsi on the mainland, near the plains of Arcadia, where there are cattle in plenty. *(Elizabethans had a passion for currants in sweet and savoury dishes. They imported over two thousand tons a year.)*

The Providore and those under him, whom they call the Signors of Health, would not allow us to come ashore because we came from Algiers where Turks live and we had some Turks on our ship from there. After six days we were given 'pratique', which means permission to disembark. The rule is that unless they have a letter of health from a Venetian or an Italian, all those who come from any part of Turkey, must remain on board ship for ten days or in the prison that they call the lazaretto. If in that time anyone happens to fall ill they all have to stay there for another ten days and again for another ten days until everyone is healthy.

GREEK EASTER

While we lay before the town for six days I noticed a hill close to the sea, which I thought would be a very good place to get a view of the whole island and the sea around it. It looked very green with open ground on top and a white thing like a rock in the middle. I liked looking at it so much that I made a kind of vow or promise that as soon as I set foot on land I would neither eat nor drink until I made it to the top. Meanwhile I worked on two of my companions and persuaded them to keep me company. One of them was Michael Watson, my carpenter, and the other Edward Hale, a coachman. When the day came to go ashore I held my companions to their promise and got them to go with me before we went into the town. The Greeks call the hill Scopo. It is more than a mile from town but I gave our sailors something to take us in the cook's boat to the foot of the mountain, as we thought. But when we came ashore we found it was almost two miles away. When we came to the foot of it, by great fortune we happened to find the right path, which was very narrow and twisting.

It was early in the morning. A couple of days before we were told not to take any weapons with us when we went ashore, so we only had cudgels. After about half a mile we looked up and saw on a ridge above us a man carrying a long staff with a clubbed end on his shoulder. On his head he wore a cape with what looked like five horns sticking up. A large herd of goats and sheep followed him. When he saw him my friend Michael Watson was very afraid and tried to persuade us to go no further, saying that the inhabitants were savages and could easily do us harm, as we had no swords or daggers or anyone else with us. But I told him that even if they were wicked men I would, with God's help, be as good as my word. Without more ado we got him to go to the ridge where we saw that the man with the club was a herdsman. Nevertheless Michael Watson swore he would go no further, come what may. Edward Hale said, without much conviction, that he would not leave me but see it to the end.

So the two of us carried on and when we were almost at the top we saw two horses grazing, with pack saddles on their backs, and a man coming down towards us with nothing in his hands. I said to my friend

"Ned, we'll see from this man what sort of people live here."

The man came up to us and put his hand on his breast and bowed and smiled. He beckoned to us to carry on up. Ned Hall tried to persuade me not to go any further but I told him it would break my oath to go back until I had been as far as I could. I came to the top where there was a pretty meadow and on one side a white house built of cement which had been the cell of a hermit, who, as I heard later, died a short time before we came and was five hundred years old. Straight ahead of us on the other side of the grass I saw a house some twenty paces long with a wall about three foot high and then open another three foot to the eaves. I saw a man on the inside pass a copper kettle out to a man on the outside. I said to Ned Hale

"I'm going over to that house to get something to drink. I am very thirsty."

The weather was very hot and I hadn't had breakfast. But Ned said it was not a good idea to take anything to drink from them or to go anywhere near them. Still, I went boldly up to the side of the house, where I saw another man drinking, and signalled that I would like something to drink. He picked up the kettle, which had water in it, and offered it to me. When I put out my hands to take it he wouldn't give it to me and put it down out of reach. He came back to the wall and lifted up a carpet on the ground. Underneath were six bottles of good wine and a beautiful silver cup. He filled it with red wine they call Robola and gave it to me. I took it and called my friend Ned, who was standing away off, afraid to come near.

"Here, Ned," I said, "a toast to all our friends in England."

"Mind what you're doing," he said, "are you going to take their drink?"

"Indeed I am. It's better than I deserve."

I thanked God for it and drank it down and it was the best wine I ever tasted. Then he filled my cup with white Robola and it was better than the red. After I praised the wine and told Ned he was a fool to turn it down he came nearer the house. He wanted some water and took it out of the kettle. When we finished I was so grateful for their hospitality that I didn't know how to thank the man. I had only half a dollar of Spanish money with me, which is the most acceptable currency in that region. I offered him the silver coin but he would not take it. Then I remembered I had two Seville knives in my pocket. I took one of them out and gave it to him. It had a gilded and engraved blade. He took it out of the sheath and looked at it and shouted "Sisto! Sisto!" in a loud voice. Another man came running and he showed him the handle. They started to wrestle for the knife but the one I gave it to kept hold of it and jumped over the wall to the side where I was. He bowed to me and took my hand and led me around the end of the house and through a little cloister into a chapel where we found a priest saying mass and wax candles burning. He sat me down in a pew, where I watched what the people did. There were about twenty men but no women, who were in a lower chapel by themselves, but they could still hear and see what was going on. Ned Hale came in but he didn't see me and knelt down near the women, who he didn't notice. But they saw him and were surprised at what he was doing. I got up from my knees to look for him and saw two women laughing at him, as well they might, for he was making a fool of himself. Neither he nor I had ever seen any part of a mass before and we were none the wiser now. The chapel was very elaborately painted and decorated in a way I had never seen before.

When the service was over we left the chapel but someone came after us and made us go back in again. He led us through the chapel and into the cloister where we found eight very pretty women, richly dressed, some in red satin, some in white and some in light blue silk. They had ornate headdresses, strings of pearls and jewelled earrings. Seven of them were young while the eighth was old and dressed all in black. I thought at first they were nuns but soon found out they were not. We were then taken into the house where I had drunk the wine. The table was laid and we were invited to sit down. They served us good bread and excellent wine and red eggs. *(Eggs dyed red for Easter. This is Easter Saturday. The women would still be fasting.)* My friend Ned would not eat or drink anything but water but I had an egg, bread and cheese and drank two bowls of wine. While we sat there the ladies came in and three of them sat down very close to us and stared at us. I offered the cup to one of them but she would not drink.

I offered my half dollar to the man who waited on us but he would not take any money. We thought that the women standing round us must live there because they would not take anything either. I gave my other knife, worth two shillings, to the old woman. She would not take it at first but then changed her mind. They all huddled round to admire it. After they had had a good look it they came up to me together and bowed to show their gratitude.

So Ned Hale and I left in very good spirits. When we got back to where we had left our faint-hearted friend Michael Watson, who had been hiding in a bush all this time, he would not believe us when we told him about the marvellous things we had seen and how well we were treated. He was ashamed of himself and wanted to hurry down to the town to get something to eat. For all that we took our time and went to see another monastery. Instead of scrub there were lots of wild flowers, thyme and other good herbs. Springs ran down into Zakynthos town.

We asked for the house where our merchants and the other passengers were staying, which was at the sign of the White Horse. Michael Watson was too embarrassed to go in with us. When our merchants saw us they were very angry, saying they had looked everywhere for us and thought we had were drowned or come to some other harm. I asked them to be quiet while I told them my adventures. When I finished my story they were amazed at my bravery and some Greeks said they had never heard of any Englishman going up there. It was then about twelve o'clock and nine of the gentlemen wanted to go straight away to see for themselves. I did not want to go up there again. I was tired and it was four miles away. They hired a guide but when they got to the mountain they missed the right path and climbed up rocks. Some of them fell and barked their shins. Eventually they got there and as I had already prepared the ground they were made very welcome. Their guide told them something that never occurred to me, which was to go into the chapel as soon as they got there and put some money in the box, as little as they liked, and then they would be well treated. They returned safely late in the evening and thanked me for what they had seen.

April 30th

With three others I went with a Greek who showed us the way to the castle.

SPORTS DAY

May 1st

On May Day we saw their biggest sports meeting of the year. The men of the Greek community meet in Zakynthos town with their best horses and weapons. They have only lances for tilting at the ring and the quintain. They borrowed our five trumpeters to herald the prizes. How they did it was so simple it is not worth recording. In the morning they ran at the ring and in the afternoon the quintain.

(The quintain was a solid target set up on a post. The ring was similar, meant to be carried off by the lance.)

THE AEGEAN

May 2nd

We left Zakynthos. The Turkish passengers from Algiers to Iskenderun, were impatient to get under way and, the wind being fair, we set sail. We went close to the island of Strophades and saw a castle. In the castle or a monastery near it there are always thirty monks. No women are allowed on the island and there are no other houses. It is low and flat and a little above a mile in length.

May 3rd

We sailed between the mainland of Greece and the lovely island of Kithira. They say that beautiful Helen was born on this island and stolen away from there before the destruction of Troy. *(An abbreviated and unconventional version.)*

May 4th

With only a light wind we sailed close to the coast of Crete. It is two hundred miles long. We sailed past a hill where St Paul preached. An old Jew, a fellow passenger, told us that on top of the hill stood the bronze statue of a man holding a strung bow and shouting to the east, which was put there by magic. Before then the east winds were so furious that few ships could survive in these waters but since then they have been like the sea everywhere else. *(A distorted version of the myth of the bronze giant Talos, given by Hephaestus to Europa to protect her from kidnap.)* We passed many little islands close to Crete, including Milos and Antimilos on the east side.

May 6th

At eleven o'clock we made a straight run between two islands no more than a length from the shore on either side. They are very high and steep mountains. On the right was Kasos, which is not inhabited and on the other side Karpathos which is. There are a lot of birds on the island, which at night roost on the ground like our wheatears in England. Sixty miles further on is the island of Rhodes. Since the island was taken by the Turks the roadstead has been kept by the Spaniards of Malta. *(Wheatears is a guess for Dallam's 'counis'. Conies are rabbits and wheatears nest in deserted rabbit burrows.)*

May 7th

We saw the coast of southern Turkey.

May 8th, 9th

We were almost becalmed

May 10th, 11th, 12th

We sailed along the coast of Cyprus, leaving it to the left. On the west side we saw the town of Paphos. Thirty miles further on, at Cape Gata, we set a man ashore who was a Greek born in Cyprus. He had a brother living in Crete, whom he had not seen for a long time. He took a ship to Crete but the wind prevented him landing and carried him to Zakynthos. In three months he did not find a single ship to take him back to Crete. When our ship came in and hearing that we were to sail past Crete he fell at our captain's feet and begged to be taken there. He was taken on board but as we sailed along the coast of Crete our captain would not let him land but took him to Cyprus, where he put him ashore. I thought this was hard luck and he thought so too, for he wept bitterly that he could not see his brother, whom he loved dearly.

About forty miles from the eastern end of the island near Cape Greko is a large town called Famagusta with a good harbour. Most of their galleys and other ships are moored there.

May 13th

We got no further than the east side of Cyprus because the wind was so light. Of all those I have seen, this island is the most pleasant. The coastline is low and open fields rise higher and higher inland so you can see nearly twenty miles. We saw a lot of wild pig. Without a doubt it is a very fertile country. When we were half way along the coast we saw Mount Lebanon in Syria, which is only two short days' journey from Jerusalem.

May 14th

With a fresh wind we rounded the cape Ras el Khanzir, which is near Iskenderun.

ISKENDERUN

May 15th

We anchored in the roadstead before Iskenderun, which is as far up the straits as a ship can go.

May 16th

Our master gunner, two of his mates, Mr Chancy our surgeon, one of our trumpeters, my mate John Harvey and I armed ourselves with musket and shot and went ashore. The mountains are so high that no ship dares go within two miles of the shore for fear of not having a wind to take them out again. The land between the mountains and the sea is deserted, with thick woods and marshes where lots of wildfowl breed along with other wild animals like pigs and foxes. We went into the woods to shoot birds. We had a lot of trouble finding a path so we would not tear our clothes. Every two or three boat-lengths we found a local hidden in a bush with a bow and arrows or a gun, which we supposed were for shooting game. We wandered some three miles through the wilderness and came across a clearing that was just a quagmire. In the middle were two massive buffaloes, bigger than our great oxen. At first we saw nothing but their heads. They made a great noise with their snuffling and then ran away, which was amazing, for if they had been oxen or cows or horses like ours, they would definitely have drowned.

While we watched them, we noticed about forty of the afore-mentioned locals getting together and trying to surround us. We could not think how to defend ourselves except by running away. The trees between us and the sea were so tall that we could not see the sea or our ship's mast. We ran pell mell through thick and thin, with thorns and briars tearing our clothes, until at last we came out into a clearing where we could see our ship a mile from the shore. We were very relieved. We relaxed beside a spring of good water, for we had nothing to eat and were exhausted by our exertions.

After we had cooled off and refreshed ourselves we returned along the seafront and the foundations of the original city of Iskenderun, as the Turks call it, previously known as Alexandretta. We saw the ruined walls of substantial houses and monasteries where there are now only bogs and ponds, and a castle so sunken and surrounded by water you cannot get into it. We saw on the walls of an old house very strange animals running up and down very fast, some of them bigger than a giant toad and the same colour, with long tails like rats. A few were long and thin but the rest were all shapes and sizes. On another occasion my mate Harvey and I went into the fields to wash our shirts and, while they were drying, went to pick fruit - there is a lot of fruit around that is free for anyone to pick - from a white damson tree. While we were busy at it we saw a great adder in the branches at least twelve or fourteen feet from the ground, and ready to pounce on us. We turned to run away and he jumped out of the tree and slithered into a briar thicket. There were many such minor incidents which I won't record.

May 18th

Our ship was meant to unload cargo for Aleppo but in the morning, when we got up, we saw an incredible number of tents on the mountainside down to the spring I mentioned before. When our captain saw this he sent a boat to discover the reason. Our merchants told him he should in no circumstances put any goods or any man ashore until he saw that all the tents were gone. They belonged to soldiers from Damascus, part of the great Turkish army, that was going to war. They would take anything on the shore that took their fancy. At night we saw them strike camp, for it is a hot country and they travel by night. Every night for four days a different contingent arrived and we stayed on board ship. Every day a great troop of splendid cavalry rode down to the sea with their lances. Some had black slaves to carry their lances and other weapons. Someone said they were ordered to Constantinople, twenty days from Iskenderun.

May 30th

The French consul at Aleppo had dinner on board our ship. The same evening our men began to unload the goods for Aleppo. They could not do it earlier because of all the janissaries who passed this way and pitched their tents within a mile and a half of the roadstead. There are few amenities and only three inns, Italian, French and English. There are some little cottages made of reeds, like summer houses, and two little tents.

June 1st

There was an unusual delivery of letters from Aleppo, seventy two miles away. After I had been there a while I realised it was quite normal. We were sitting talking in our merchants' house and pigeons were pecking around us. A white dove flew in and landed on the ground with the others. One of the merchants said "Welcome Honest Tom" and picked him up. A letter the size of a shilling was tied under his wing with thread and dated only four hours before. I saw this happen again and the letters always arrived four hours after they were sent.

June 4th

In the morning more than twenty tents were pitched in the same place as before. I could not find out how many janissaries there were since I could not talk to them or anyone else who knew. Most were horsemen, all with a lance and most of them had a slave to carry it. Each had a bow and arrows and a scimitar at his side. The way they shoot and their bows and arrows are different from ours.

Our longboat went every Friday to buy food in the market at Tarsus, where St Paul was born, only sixteen miles from Iskenderun. About half way, slightly closer to Iskenderun, is the rock where the Greeks and Turks say Jonas was spewed out from the belly of the whale. Our master gunner, one of his mates, my mate and I, with two sailors to row us, went there to gather a sackful of samphire.

RHODES

June 10th

We left Iskenderun for Constantinople with the wind against us so we had to tack from shore to shore. Towards evening we came near a fine town on our right, stretching a long way along the coast. At one end is a large castle. It is called Ayas and is about twenty four miles from Tarsus, which the Turks call Bayas. They change the names of most of their towns.

June 12th, 13th, 14th

We sailed along the coast of Asia Minor. The wind was unfavourable so we had plenty of time to look at the coastline.

June 15th

We saw Cyprus again.

June 20th

We rounded a cape a hundred miles from Iskenderun.

June 23rd

We sailed past Kastelorizo in Asia Minor.

June 25th

In the distance we saw the famous island of Rhodes, which in the past was held by Christian knights and is now inhabited by Turks.

June 26th

We sailed along the coast of Rhodes and had a good enough view of it because the wind was directly against us. We could see several forts on little mountains. The island is sixty miles long and sixteen miles wide.

June 27th

Today Thomas Cable died. He was under twenty years old and the son of one of the owners of our ship.

As we were due to pass between the north end of the island and the coast of Asia, which is only twenty miles, and the wind in the gulf was against us, and we also needed fresh water and our provisions were running low, our captain and merchants thought it a good idea to call in at the town of Rhodes. As we came to an anchorage near the town walls we saw in the roadstead a Turkish galleon, their biggest ship of about a thousand tons. It was a frail-looking tub yet she had a rich cargo from Alexandria. We had no sooner dropped anchor than Turks started to board us. That first day no fewer than five hundred rude Turks came on board and again on every day that we stayed there.

June 28th

The Captain Pasha, governor of the town, had gone away with the galleys on important business. His Deputy, who had taken over his responsibilities, came on board with the chief men of the town. The ship was decked out as handsomely as possible in the time. Our gun-room was one of the best rooms in the ship and made a good impression. I kept my harpsichord in the gun-room and our master gunner asked me to open it. The Turks and Jews who came in saw it and wondered what it could be. When I sat down and played they were astounded. Several of them tried to hug me and kiss me and wanted me to come and live with them. After the Deputy had toured the ship our captain gave him enough broadcloth to make the Captain Pasha a coat or a gown. And so they left.

As soon as they were gone, the ship's steward and his men, my mate Harvey and I went ashore to see the town. I examined the gate and saw an inscription carved in the stone. All I could make out was the year when it was built or restored, 1475. We went through the gate and turned first right up a very handsome street towards the walls. There we found massive guns of brass and iron made by Christians. A few of the great brass canon exploded when the Turks besieged the town. Some cannon were made of hammered iron staves, each about three inches square and hooped around like a barrel. The bore was big enough for two men to get in together. Our Greek guide told us that when one of these cannons were fired it took at least two hours to reload it. The town has double walls, the length of a couple of boat-lengths between them. The ditch in between is very deep but dry.

The city wall facing the sea is incredibly massive and armed with cannon not on top of the wall but sticking through it. They are positioned that no ship can pass on that side without permission. In most of the streets inside the town you cannot trot a horse, for they are paved with marble cobbles of all sizes from sixteen inches to three inches. There are many other things about the city and the island that I will not record until I get back to England. But of all the towns and cities I have ever seen, I have never seen the like for fortifications.

We wasted no time. We made a circuit of the walls without stopping, except to drink a jug of wine that cost only a penny. We hurried to the seafront to get back on board. When we were outside the gate we looked for our boat and saw it coming from the ship with Mr Maye our preacher, and our ambassador's under-butler. Mr Maye said to me

"Are you going back to the ship?"

"Yes indeed, I am very hungry and I am tired of walking."

"Please, come back with me to the gate so I can see the inscription above it and step inside and then I will go back with you," he said.

So we all went back with Mr Maye to the gate. When we got there he saw a water fountain like one of our drinking fountains with a polished steel cup hanging on a chain, for the Turks drink only water.

"Please, come with me to that fountain over there for a drink of water." he said, "It looks good and I would like to taste it."

So we went with him to the fountain and we all had a cup of water. While we were drinking, two haughty-looking Turks came up and said to Mr Maye "Parly Franco Signor," which means "do you speak Italian Signor?"

While they were talking I looked round and saw a Turk sitting in his shop, who knew me. He heard me play the keyboard on the ship and hugged me. He beckoned

me over and when I got close, signalled to me to be gone
and pointed to the gate and told me to hurry. So I made
off as fast as I could. My mate Harvey and the rest of us
followed as fast as they could, leaving Mr Maye and the
under-butler talking with the Turks, for they could speak
a bit of Italian and none of us could. Outside the gate we
looked back to the fountain but saw nobody there. The
Turks had taken the two of them off to prison.
Fortunately we found our boat and the sailors were ready
to leave. As soon as I got on board our ship I went to the
captain and told him everything that had happened.
When I told him I had been in town he imagined that we
had somehow given offence. It is dangerous for foreign
Christians to look round the town and he thought it was
our fault the two were arrested. I will not repeat what I
said to him until we get back to England. For the rest of
the day nobody was brave enough to go ashore and
nobody came on board.

The next morning a little Greek boat came from the
town with a letter from Mr Maye addressed to our
captain and merchants and the whole of the crew. It was
so pitiful you would think they had been in prison seven
years. It told how they were taken from the fountain tied
together like two dogs with a rusty chain and thrown into
a dark dungeon, where they were fastened to a ring on a
post. They had to stay on their feet and could not sit or
kneel. Every two hours their captors shook wire whips at
them and threatened them with cruel punishments. They
begged us to get them released as soon as possible or else
they might be put to death. They would not be able to
endure the miserable conditions and the torture that

would probably be inflicted on them as soon as the ship set sail. Our captain and the merchants were so upset by this letter and sympathetic to the prisoners' plight that they put aside their fear and decided to go ashore.

Our captain and five merchants plucked up courage and went bravely to the Captain Pasha's house. They asked to speak with his deputy the Deputy. He made them wait for a time and then came out to ask why they had come. One of our men who spoke the best Italian told him that they were very much aggrieved that two of their men had been detained in prison without being told the reason. They were astonished that they were so bold as to arrest any of our men when we were carrying such a valuable gift to the Sultan. The two men they had detained were most distinguished, one being our preacher the other being in charge of the Present. They said this and other things to intimidate them. They also said that if he would not hand over the men immediately they would hire a galley and send word to the Sultan to explain how they had been wronged and their journey delayed without explanation. The Deputy replied

"Yesterday I was on board your ship representing the Captain Pasha in his absence. You did not entertain me in a way befitting my position. You did not give me dinner nor did you give me a present for the Captain Pasha."

Our men replied

"We entertained you the best we could in the time you gave us. We could not give you dinner because we had nothing even for ourselves. We came here to rest from our journey and to buy what provisions we could get for our money. It is not true that you did not have a present for the Captain Pasha. You had enough broadcloth to make your Captain a coat."

The Deputy said "I had none for myself and I want some before you can have your men back."

Our men replied "Is that the only thing that caused you to imprison our men? If we give you a present will you release them?"

"Of course," said the Deputy. And so the dispute was ended. Now you can see the mean and greedy character of those barbarous and cruel Turks and how they look down on Christians.

June 30th

Having freed our men from prison we weighed anchor, hoisted sail and set off.

THE DODECANESE

July 1st

We entered the Aegean and sailed through the Dodecanese and its wonderful cluster of little islands.

July 2nd

We left Kos to the south. The north coast is very pleasant lowland stocked with vines and plenty of other fruit. We saw a lovely town, whose walls defy the waves. Inside the walls are fine houses, which were not built by Turks although they now enjoy them. We happened to drop anchor for the night before the town but set sail in the morning. The town is also called Kos.

July 3rd

Standing on the upper deck I counted no fewer than six islands around us.

July 4th

Leaving Leros to the south we came to Samos, birthplace of the famous philosopher Pythagoras. The island is mostly inhabited by Greeks. As the wind was against us and we found a good roadstead we moored in sight of a little town a mile or more from the coast. As soon as we dropped anchor we saw the townspeople run into the fields and drive their livestock as fast as they could up into the mountains. There was another little ship anchored half a mile away from us which they hauled ashore and unloaded. But they need not have taken so much trouble because we meant them no harm.

An hour after nightfall we weighed anchor but the wind was dead ahead in the narrow passage between two islands so we had to put in again at the south-east corner of Samos under a huge mountain. I think it is made of nothing but pumice and certainly the side nearest the sea is solid rock and rises vertical.

July 5th

Some of our men went ashore to look for fresh water and firewood. One of them, a bold lad, stole away from his mates and went into the town. He assumed he could make himself understood. The rest of them came back on board without him, thinking he had been taken prisoner. The next day, at about ten o'clock, he came to the shore and waved for a boat. He brought with him some chickens and bread and was half drunk on wine. About two hours later the governor of the island, a Turk, came to the shore with a present, hoping to get a better one in return.

They grow a kind of corn they call millet, with small seed like canary-seed. When sown it yields a hundred and fifty fold. The bread they make with it is finer than wheat bread.

July 8th

John Knill died, servant of Mr Wiseman, a merchant and one of the owners of the ship.

July 10th

We weighed anchor and tried to follow a course between two islands but the wind would not let us, being from the north-west as before. Seeing we could not make headway we came back to the place where we first anchored, thinking we could get some fresh provisions and water. But it was dark before we could get into harbour and due to the negligence of the sailor taking the soundings the ship ran aground, which made us very anxious all night. In the end all was well.

July 11th

In the morning we planned to go ashore but we saw four galleys and a frigate creeping along the coast. The galleys remained about four miles away, by the Asia

Minor coast, but the frigate came into the roadstead to see who we were and dropped anchor. Not knowing their intentions our captain gave orders to weigh anchor with all speed. Already under sail the frigate and the galleys were in front of us. So our captain decided on a course he would not have dared before. Instead of leaving the island on our right now we left it on our left and went between Samos and the mainland of Asia Minor. It is an incredibly narrow passage for a ship such as ours. Even at its narrowest the four galleys stayed with us but when they saw our armaments and our determination they were afraid of us. They positioned the galleys close to the shore so their beaks or their oars touched the land and we had scarcely enough room to pass between them and the mainland. Our captain called us all on deck to make as much of a show of strength as we could and as soon as we were beside them our five trumpets blew, to their surprise. They looked hard at us but said nothing. So we faced them down when they meant to intimidate us and left them behind on the coast of Samos..

July 12th
    Chios came in view. We sailed past the coast

CHIOS

July 14th
    We dropped anchor in a roadstead eight miles away from the great town of Chios.

July 15th

Our long boat was made ready to go ashore for fresh water which we sorely needed since for three days we had nothing to eat but rice boiled in fetid water and our drinking water also stank. As soon as it was launched, three of our gentleman passengers came and asked me if I would go ashore with them to see if we could buy some fresh provisions. I said I would. When we were in the boat the captain was told of it. He looked over the side and spoke to me. He was happy to let the others go and never come back and he would not have waited half an hour for them. But they knew that he would not leave me behind. The captain asked if I wanted to go and I said I only wanted to get ashore, drink some fresh water and take the boat back again. He told me to come back on board right away but the gentlemen held me tight. Nor did I want to obey his order.

"Very well," said the captain," I see you want to go ashore and your friends will take you up to that town you can see over there. Just let me tell you before you go what you can expect. Mastic grows nowhere in the world except on this island and now is the season. The only commodities here are mastic, cotton and wine. The only way to get to the town is through gardens where these things grow. If they see you taking a single sprig of mastic or a single boll of cotton or a single bunch of grapes you will go to prison for a whole year without remission. Don't say I didn't warn you."

After the captain told us of the dangers we could fall into unawares he said that if I did not come back with the boat as soon as she had taken on water he would set sail and be gone. We had no fear of that and as soon as we landed went straight to the town. It is two miles from the sea. From a distance it looked pretty with a castle in the middle.

It was Sunday. The people had rarely seen anything like our ship before. As soon as we came ashore a lot of women and children came down to meet us and we were as much a curiosity to them as they were to us. We carried straight on without a word until we came to the town centre by the castle wall and stood looking around us. A Greek came up and asked who we were looking for and where we wanted to go. Two of us spoke good Italian and said that we wanted to buy provisions. He said there was a consul in the town and we had to report to him before we could buy anything. He took us to the consul's house. The streets were full of people staring at us.

When we got to the consul's house we had to go up some outside stairs to a veranda at the back of the house that looked out to sea where our ship lay at anchor. The consul was sitting at table with six well-dressed and beautiful women. As soon as we came up the women left and the consul stood up to embrace us and say we were most welcome. He had the table laid with a fine spread of delicacies and only two little loaves of bread. He gave us an excellent red wine. While we were sitting there talking the townspeople came up to the walls of the consul's garden which was on that side. They were so keen to see us that they climbed on the dry stone walls. The consul stood up several times and shouted at them and waved his hands and threatened punishment but the more he shouted at them the more people climbed on the wall until it gave way. It collapsed with a great noise the length of a couple of boats and as much again in another place. This made the consul very angry and he might well have wished we hadn't come.

From where we were sitting we could see our ship in front of us and the boat going alongside with water. Meanwhile the consul sent two men into town to see what provisions they could get for us. After two hours they came back and said that all they could find for sale, as it was Sunday, was a bushel of garlic. We were happy to take it so at least we had something. We saw we were a nuisance to the consul so we took our leave. He told one of the men to carry our garlic for us. As we went down the stairs from the veranda the leading ladies of the town were on the steps one above the other to see us off. They stood so we could see their faces and bare bosoms. They were richly dressed with jewelled necklaces and earrings and their hair very prettily done with different coloured ribbons. What most impressed us was their beauty and their clear complexions. I think that nowhere in the world can compare with the women in these parts for looks.

Afterwards we were told that if we had gone to the city six miles further on we would have been much better entertained by the English consul Mr William Aldridge, a fine gentleman. But our captain would not put in there in case he was put to any expense. For he was a very mean and miserly man, always out for his own profit, and not interested in what other people wanted or the welfare of his passengers.

Back on board no-one turned their nose up at our bag of garlic and we could have sold it at a profit.

The same day we weighed anchor and set sail but to little purpose and before morning we dropped it again in almost the same place.

THE DARDANELLES

July 16th

We weighed anchor again and were becalmed very close to the city of Chios but our captain would not let anyone go ashore.

July 19th

We came to the island of Tenedos, directly opposite the south end of the plain and ruins of the great city of Troy. The wind was dead against us and there is also a powerful current that comes from the Dardanelles. We dropped anchor near the south gate of Troy. A large part of the gate is still standing along with massive remains of the great walls of old. *(Not Troy, which remained buried for the next four hundred years, but Alexandria Troas.)*

July 20th

We weighed anchor again but could get no further for the wind and the current were against us and we dropped it again in the same place.

July 21st

A boy called John Felton died. He was born in Yarmouth.

I went ashore with a few of the others and saw some of the monuments of Troy - remains of the walls, carvings and marble columns. When we got back on board eleven of the Sultan's galleys came rowing and sailing past. To stop them coming aboard our captain ordered the anchor weighed. Towards evening when the wind failed we anchored again.

July 22nd

Two frigates came down the Dardanelles. Seeing that we were English from the flag on our maintop, two Englishmen in one of them asked their captain to hail us, which he was happy to do. When our captain saw this and that the frigates were Turkish, he ordered the anchor weighed immediately so they could not come aboard. When they come on board Turkish captains usually demand a present or try to cadge something. So by the time they came alongside we were under sail. The two Englishmen hailed us and after the usual greetings told our captain that the Admiral of the Sultan's navy was approaching with fifteen galleys. We would recognise the flagship by two lanterns on the poop deck while the others had only one. With that the frigates left us.

No sooner had the frigates gone when we spotted the galleys coming down the Dardanelles towards us along the walls of Troy. They were a marvellous sight, decorated with beautiful paintwork and excellent varnish. The slaves rowing them were all naked. As they were rowing towards Tenedos the wind turned fair so they hoisted sails and spread a canvas over the slaves. When the galleys were under sail they made an even better show than before. The sails were made of cotton, one white and the other blue, with masts of the same colours. As they passed by, our captain ordered a three gun salute which was poorly done. But being so near the walls of Troy, the echo was such that every gun sounded like five. The Admiral sent a galley to demand his present and to ask why we had not given him a better salute. Our captain replied that the admiral's present was sealed under the hatches. He would not know what it was until we met our ambassador in Constantinople. And the reason why we had not given more of a salute was that he did not know that the Admiral was on board. If he had known he would have fired every gun on the ship.

After these excuses the men in the little boat that came alongside us said that their captain could not go back to his Admiral without a small present. Our captain made a thorough search of the ship and found two Dutch chests, which he sent to the Admiral. Then the captain of the galley demanded a present for himself. Our captain said he had nothing to give. The galley captain asked for tobacco and pipes, which our captain gave him. He went over to Tenedos where the Admiral and the other galleys had dropped anchor. As he left our captain gave him a one-gun salute.

About two hours after the galley had gone a light wind took us only as far as Cape Janissary. I went ashore there with some of our merchants. We found a scattered little village inhabited by Greeks and bought bread and chickens. We saw more ruined walls and houses of Troy. I took away a piece of white marble pillar which I broke off with a hammer that my mate Harvey brought ashore for this purpose. I brought this piece of marble back to London. Cape Janissary is about ten miles from Tenedos.

We went back on board ship and set sail the same day. We sailed thirty miles up the Dardanelles and dropped anchor near two castles by the name of Sestos and Abydos. Sestos is in Thrace and Abydos opposite in Asia Minor. They are well fortified for the defence of the Dardanelles, through which all shipping en route to Constantinople has to pass. The commander of one of the castles came on board our ship with a present. Other commanders came on board while we were there as well as the consul of Gallipoli who happened to be passing by. He is a friar and and a very fine gentleman.

GALLIPOLI

August 4th

While we waited for a wind we often went ashore but I will pass over what we did and what we saw.

Our ambassador, who was in Constantinople, heard that our ship was waiting for a wind and sent down a slave row-boat to fetch letters and those of us with the Sultan's Present. Mr Thomas Glover, Mr Bailey of Salisbury and a janissary came down in it. We were about 250 miles from Constantinople.

August 5th

As well as those connected with the Present, our preacher Mr Maye and other gentlemen, who had come to serve the ambassador, had to leave the ship and go with us, since our physicians thought that one of our sailors was infected with the plague. The row-boat could not take all of us so Mr Glover hired two more. We were sixteen in all, including Mr Glover and Mr Bailey.

August 6th

We arrived at Gallipoli and went to the house of the Italian consul, who is a friar. He was very hospitable but we did not have time to see the city. We had a favourable wind and were anxious to set off again. In the middle of the following night we had no wind at all and the crew was tired with rowing, so we went ashore. We found three or four windmills and the walls of an old castle. Although it was very dark, some of our men rowed up and down until they found a little cottage, where they got fire. Others broke up an old hedge and we made a big fire under the castle wall. In Gallipoli, the day before, we had bought a side of mutton. We stewed half of it and roasted the rest. It was a simple meal but we enjoyed it and were warm enough with our big fire. We set off again before morning.

August 7th

At daybreak the wind came up so strong that we had to land and haul our boats up at a large town called Eriklici. We found plenty of wine and bread and some of our party went into the fields and vineyards to pick grapes. They were chased off by the Greeks who owned them and were in danger of physical injury and of losing their clothes. Cuthbert Bull lost his cloak and the ambassador's cook was caught and his belt and knives taken off him. Big Mr Gonzale got them all back again and chased off the Greeks, beating them with their own weapons, although not on their own property. Then the poor Greeks complained to the town governor, who was with us and had given us a sheep. He quickly made peace among us and Mr Glover was happy to compensate the Greeks for their trouble.

The town governor is very imposing and well-built but not very athletic. Some of us took him on at various sports. He could not run, jump, wrestle, toss the caber, putt the shot, throw the hammer or fight with cudgel or sword. But if he got his arms round a man he would crush him so his chest hurt and he couldn't breathe. When he was asked why he could not do the other exercises he said that Turks never did them, unlike the Christians.

We spent the night in the town. The next morning our leader Mr Glover gave the governor two or three gold pieces of gold they call sequins, worth nine shillings a piece, for his kindness and good company. He was anxious to to give us a good time and sorry to see us go.

August 8th

We continued our journey by land, towing our boats ten miles along the shore. In the afternoon we came to a town called Hora or Hosköy Our boats could go no further as the wind was too strong and the sea too rough. We stayed the night there.

Here and especially at the previous town, there are a lot of cornfields and vineyards as well as quantities of silkworms. A jug of wine is a penny. However the inhabitants are very poor because the Turks oppress them, taxing the fruit of the poor people's labour.

The area we travelled through, opposite Troy, where we left our ship, is Thrace, where Constantinople is situated.

NIGHT ALARM

August 9th

We left our boats at Hora and went three miles to the town of Ganos. We could not go any further along the sea for it is so hilly and wooded, a veritable wilderness. So we spent the day and the night there on the lookout for our boats, but they did not come. We had a good look around the town and did not think much of the people's living conditions so our leader, Mr Glover, found a house for us to stay in near the shore. The town was on a hill and this house was on a cliff the height of St Paul's overlooking the sea. We had to go up a ladder onto a balcony built on the side of the house with a little door into a room with only bare boards to sleep on. For the whole time we were on the road we never took off our clothes or found a bed to sleep in. In this room there was not so much as a stool or a bench to sit on or anything else except a shelf with two jugs and two earthenware plates. There was no window and the only light came through a little hole in the stone wall.

We arrived at the town before noon and, after a quick dinner, passed the time by walking down to the edge of a wood beside the sea. It was abandoned and unexploited by the look of it. We saw many wild animals that we do not have in England. As it was getting dark and remembering how hard the beds were in our new hostelry, we found thick, soft vegetation at the edge of the wood. Every one of us gathered a bundle of it to sleep on.

When night fell and we had had our supper every man chalked his place on the bare boards. Our janissary chose a board that was loose on the joists. We all kept our swords beside us. Two of us had muskets. We had been lying down for half an hour when those of us who had weed pillows were suddenly attacked by insects that bit much worse than fleas. We were glad to throw our pillows away and swept the house clean. But we could not get off to sleep. As we lay awake in that dark, uncomfortable house Mr Glover, who had lived a long time in those parts, told us about the strange animals he had seen. He talked a lot about adders, snakes and reptiles, the differences between them and how big they were.

We passed the time talking of such things until most of us fell asleep and those who could not lay quietly and said nothing so as not to disturb the others. All was quiet. Mr Bailey needed to go outside to relieve himself. The little door opened onto the balcony. The wind was blowing hard and made a lot of noise for the house was exposed to the sea and the elements. When he lay down Mr Bailey untied his garters. One of them was loose and trailed behind him and when he went onto the balcony the wind blew it round the other leg. It was a long silk garter and the strong wind wrapped it round his legs. Our talk of adders and snakes and reptiles was still in his mind. He imagined they swarmed around him and was convinced there was a snake round his legs. He shouted at the top of his voice "A snake! A snake! A snake!" He was so terrified he could not find the door to get back in and blundered about the balcony and made a great din. The rest of us inside the house thought he said "Attacked! Attacked!" During the day we suspected they were plotting against us in the town so now we thought the house was surrounded with men determined to cut our throats.

There were fifteen of us in that little room. It was around midnight and very dark. We seized our swords and were about to attack each other for no reason. One man could not find his sword and tried to climb up the chimney, which collapsed on top of him. Another man woke up suddenly and lashed out with his sword and knocked down the shelf with the jugs and plates and smashed them. Others thought they were pulling the house down around our heads. Startled by the sudden noise, our janissary, who was supposed to be guarding us and protecting us from danger, and who also suspected the townspeople, took up the board he was lying on and slipped down into the cellar. In the midst of the panic Mr Bailey at last found the door. Seeing him come in Mr Glover said "Hey, what's going on, who's out there?" Mr Bailey, gasping with fear and shouting and struggling to get in the door, could not answer at first. At last he said "A snake! A snake attacked me!" As soon as he heard this

Mr Glover's fears evaporated. He went outside and found Mr Bailey's garter blowing away in the wind.

We were astounded that something so trivial had caused such panic. Then Mr Glover had a roll call to see if anyone had been killed or wounded. There were sixteen of us with weapons drawn in that little room. We were all alive and with only some minor injuries. Then we discovered that our janissary was missing. He was probably embarrassed to tell us where he was. Mr Glover shouted for him several times until he answered from the cellar. There was no way he could get out. Mr Gonzale took up the board where he went down and lying on the floor just managed to reach his hand. They pulled him up without difficulty. When he jumped into the cellar he was very frightened and took off his top coat. He left it in the cellar and could not be persuaded to go down again to fetch it. It was horrible down there and it seemed he was scared of the same sort of thing that frightened Mr Bailey. His coat stayed there until morning when the owner of the house fetched it out.

CONSTANTINOPLE

August 10th

The next morning Mr Sharpe, Mr Lambert and two other gentlemen hired mules and continued by land, three days journey, to Stamboul or Constantinople. The same day, after these four gentlemen had left, we returned to Hora where we had left the boats and stayed the night there.

August 11th

We set off in the morning and in the afternoon went ashore at the town of Heraklea. On a hill between the town and the sea are twenty two fine windmills, each with six sails. They are evenly spaced in a straight line and were a fine sight from the sea. We were made most welcome at this town and enjoyed ourselves until midnight when we got back in our boats.

August 14th

We came to Silivri, a large and pretty town. We went ashore for wine and water but did not stay long enough to see the whole place. I saw a lot of musk melons as big as our citrons as well as pumpkins on sale for a penny or three halfpence each.

August 15th

Wednesday. We arrived in Constantinople.

August 16th

Our ship dropped anchor by the Seven Towers, the first port you come to. It is almost two miles from there to the Sultan's palace. The next day they started to paint her.

August 17th

We went on board to collect the Present and took it to our ambassador's house in Galata, in the vineyards of Pera. Because none of the rooms in the house had high enough ceilings he had a room built very quickly in the courtyard outside the house, where we could set up the Present and put it in perfect order before we took it to the Sultan's Seraglio, or palace.

August 20th

Monday. We started work. But when we opened the chests we discovered that all the glue work was completely perished for having lain six months in the hold of our ship. The extreme heat in the hold and the effect of the sea and the hot weather in these parts melted the glue. Also some of my metal pipes were dented and broken.

Our ambassador and Mr William Aldridge and all the other gentlemen were shocked to see what condition it was in and said it was worthless. I will not repeat what I said to the ambassador and Mr Aldridge but when Mr Aldridge heard what I said he told me that if I managed put it back in perfect condition he would give me fifteen shillings of his own money. So I set about my work.

August 23rd

The King of Fez came to see me work and sat watching me half a day.

August 27th

The King of Fez came to watch us work again. *(The Fez royal family had been driven into exile fifty years before by the Emperor of Morocco.)*

August 28th

Our ship the Hector came to salute the Sultan on the north side of the Seraglio. He was in his pavilion on the wall next to the sea. The extraordinary salute captivated the Sultan and the other Turks. The newly painted ship flew a flag from every mast-top, that is the maintop, foretop, mizzentop, and bowsprit, and sported a silk pennant from every yard-arm. I cannot describe how splendid she looked. Her waist-cloths were out and on every mast-top stood as many men with muskets as were able to fire.

They weighed anchor. It was a calm and beautiful day. When everything was ready the gunners fired over a hundred and fifty large shot and between them a volley of small shot. The discipline and timing were outstanding and they were all to be congratulated. But I have to say that to my simple mind all this pomp and gunpowder was seriously misplaced on an infidel. One of the crew, the ships' carpenter, was sick. With the noise of the first great cannon being fired he died. Also, at the very end of the performance, one of the best sailors on board was servicing a large cannon in the bow. As he rammed in his powder cartridge there was still fire in the breech. The powder exploded and blew the man away in the smoke. About three days later his bottom half from the waist down was found two miles away and his head somewhere else.

When it was over the Sultan sent two men aboard to see how many cannon we had. He thought there were eighty when in fact there were twenty-seven.

August 30th

I finished the job and put the finishing touches at the ambassador's house.

September 2nd

The Sultan wished to have a better look at our ship and sailed round it in his golden caique. He was not expected and they did not realise he had been there until two or three hours later. An hour after him his mother the Sultana came for a look in the same way. *(Sultana Safiya, born into a noble Venetian family, was a power behind two thrones, the favourite of Sultan Murat III and the mother of Mehmet III. She exchanged letters and gifts with Queen Elizabeth.)*

September 3rd

Our ambassador delivered a present to the Grand Vizier at his house.

September 4th

The Chief White Eunuch, the Kapi Aga, came to see our instrument. *(The Kapi Aga, also known as the 'Keeper of the Gate', was in charge of everything in the Seraglio up to the doors of the harem, which was the responsibility of the Chief Black Eunuch, the Kizlar Aga.)*

September 7th

The Captain of the Guard, entitled the Head Gardener, came to see it. The Patriarch was expected but he did not come as Turks were dining with the ambassador. *(The Head Gardener was a janissary. In addition to their guard duties, janissaries of the Seraglio were gardeners, boatmen, torturers and executioners. Dallam does not deign to mention the ambassador's name, Henry Lello, nicknamed 'Fog' by his colleagues. The Levant Company paid his salary, as well as those of the consuls.)*

September 8th

Saturday. We began to dismantle the instrument because today the Sultan went six miles by water from the Seraglio to another seraglio where his mother lives. For a month a year, August or September, he is allowed to go there. At other times he does not go so far from his Seraglio without a guard of some hundred thousand men.

THE SERAGLIO

September 9th

Tuesday. We transported our instrument over the water to the Seraglio, and I began to set it up in the grandest of his pavilions. We crossed from Galata to the Seraglio over the Dardanelles, the channel that comes down from the Black Sea and divides Asia and Thrace. As it comes down to Galata a branch of the channel goes inland some six miles and divides the two cities of Galata and Constantinople.*(The Golden Horn)* You can get from one to the other by land but it is twelve miles and by water it is one mile. At every gate of the Seraglio sits a massive Turk with the status of a justice of the peace, called a Doorkeeper. The gates are closed for nobody goes in or out as they please. Going in through the first gate there are five great brass cannon engraved with Christian coats of arms. Then we went down some delightful walks and gardens. The walks are lined with stately cypress trees evenly spaced. Between and behind them are smaller trees bearing excellent fruit of every kind. I will not describe the gardens now.

The path from the first gate to the second wall goes uphill a quarter of a mile or more. The gate in the second wall was also closed. My interpreter called inside to the gatekeepers. Although they knew we were coming they would not open the gates until we told them our business. The gates are made of massive iron. Two janissary cadets opened them. *(Janissaries were usually Christians from the Balkans conscripted or bought from their families at* an early age, converted and trained in soldiering, gardening, and cooking. The standard of the janissaries was a cook pot, their cap badge a rice fork and their ranks named after kitchen duties. The crack unit was called the Imperial Larder.)

Inside the first wall there is only one house belonging to the Captain of the Guard. He has a thousand cadets under him who do nothing but look after the gardens. I do not think there are any in the world so well kept. Inside the second wall there are no gardens, only grand buildings and many courtyards paved with marble and similar stone. Every alcove and corner has one or more excellent fruit trees. There is an abundance of sweet grapes of several varieties. You can pick grapes every day of the year. In November when I sat down to dinner I watched them picking grapes off the vine for me to eat. For a month I dined in the Seraglio and we had grapes every day after the main course.

The place where I was to set up the instrument looked more like a church than a house. It was actually a pleasure palace and a slaughter house. Inside the building was a little apartment, very elaborate inside and out. I have never seen the like for carving, gilding, paintwork and varnish. The present Sultan had nineteen brothers put to death in that little apartment. It was built for the sole purpose of strangling them.

The main house has two rows of marble pillars. The pedestals are made of brass and double gilt. The walls on three sides of the house only go up to the eaves and the rest is open. But if there is a storm or a gale they can quickly lower cotton hangings that will keep out any kind of weather and just as quickly open them again. The fourth side of the house is closed as it adjoins another building. The wall is made of porphyry or some such stone, and you can see yourself in it as you walk past. On the floor, as in all the other houses in the Seraglio, are rich silk carpets, each of which takes four or six men to carry. There are no chairs or tables or benches, only one royal divan. On one side is a pond full of different-coloured fish.

The ambassador sent Mr Paul Pindar, who was then his secretary, with a present for the Sultana, who was in her garden. It was a coach worth six hundred pounds. The Sultana took a great liking to Mr Pindar and afterwards asked to see him in private, but the meeting was cancelled.

September 15th

I finished my work at the Seraglio. I went back every day to check on it. I dined there almost every day for a month, which they could remember no Christian ever having done before and still remain a Christian.

September 18th

I was there rather a long time. The Kapi Aga asked me if one of his friends could hear the instrument. Before I left the two cadets who look after the house hugged me and kissed me and tried to persuade me to stay with the Sultan and work for him

September 21st

At night it was wonderful to see the number of lamps burning on all the church towers in Constantinople and Galata. When we asked the reason they told us that it was the night Mohamed their Messiah was born.

THE PRESENT

September 24th

In the evening the ambassador summoned me to his chamber and instructed me to go early next morning to the Seraglio and make the instrument as perfect as possible, for the Sultan was to come and see it before noon and he himself was to be received and present his letters. After he had given me this instruction he said he had done his official duty by informing me of mine and then said

"Because I know you will not take this unkindly I will tell you straight what will happen. You have come here with a Present from our gracious Queen, not to an ordinary prince or king but a mighty monarch of the world. It would have been better for you of it had been sent to a Christian prince for then you would have been sure of receiving a large reward for your pains. But you must remember that you have brought this valuable present not only to a monarch but also an infidel and the great enemy of all Christians. Whatever we or any other Christians bring him he thinks we owe it to him out of deference or fear or in the hope of some great favour we expect from him. He has never been known to give a reward to any Christian when receiving a present and so you must expect nothing from him. You might think that for your long and exhausting journey at the risk of your life you deserve a glimpse of him. But do not expect that either.

You have seen what great preparations we have made and continue to make since you arrived for the credit of our country and for delivering the Present and my letters, which we will do tomorrow, with God's help. We call it Kissing the Sultan's Hand. When I come to his gates I will have to dismount and be searched and escorted by two men holding my hands down to my sides into the presence of the Sultan. I must kiss his knee or his sleeve. When I have handed my letters to the Kapi Aga I will be led away backwards for as long as I can see him. I will lose my head if I turn my back on him. Therefore you must not expect to have sight of him.

I thought I should tell you this in case you blamed me afterwards or said I could have warned you. Don't let this affect your work. When you get home our merchants will thank you if the Sultan is happy with it tomorrow. I do not care about the next day. If he is not pleased with it at first sight and it doesn't do all the things he was told it would do, he will have it pulled down and trample it under his feet. And then none of our petitions will be granted and all our trouble and expense will be lost."

After I had thanked the ambassador for this friendly advice, although there was little comfort in it, I told him that I had understood as much from our merchants before I left London and he should have no fear of any shortcomings in me or my work. He had seen for himself the care and skill I dedicated to repairing perfectly what everyone thought irreparable and in fact making it better in some ways than when Her Majesty saw it in the banqueting house at Whitehall.

September 25th

I went to the Seraglio with my mate Harvey the engineer, Rowland Bucket the painter, and Michael Watson the carpenter. An hour or two later the ambassador set off for the Seraglio. He was mounted like a king, except he had no crown. Twenty-two gentlemen and merchants rode with him all dressed in gold lamé. The gentlemen were Mr Humphrey Conisby, Mr Bailey of Salisbury, Mr Paul Pindar, Mr William Aldridge, Mr Jonas Aldridge and Mr Thomas Glover. The other six were merchants. They rode in gold lamé coats. Twenty-eight more went on foot in blue Turkish-style gowns with green silk capes in the Italian style. I wore a handsome cloak of French green.

I had set everything up in full working order when the cadets who look after the house saw the Sultan coming over the water in his golden caique. He had come six miles that morning. From where I stood I saw him set foot on land. The cadets told me I had to leave the house because the Sultan would soon be here. It was almost half a mile between the water and the house but the Sultan was keen to see the Present and came quickly. My mates and I were ushered out and the door locked behind us. I heard another door open and suddenly a loud noise of people coming in. For a moment it seemed that when the Sultan arrived, the door which I heard opening suddenly liberated four hundred people who had been locked up in his absence. Set free, they voiced their amazement at the first sight of the Present.

The Sultan sat down on his great throne and commanded silence. As soon as everybody stopped talking and there was absolute silence, the Present began to salute the Sultan. When I left I allowed a quarter of an hour for him to get there. First the clock struck twenty two. *(Constantinople had a twenty four hour system, probably starting at the noon prayer. In this case the presentation would have been at ten o'clock in the morning.)* Then a chime of sixteen bells started to play a four part melody. When they had finished, two figures standing on the second storey holding silver trumpets raised them to their lips and blew a fanfare. Then the music started with a five part song played twice. At the top of the organ, which was sixteen foot tall, there was a holly bush full of blackbirds and thrushes which sang and flapped their wings when the music was over. There were various other movements which amazed the Sultan. He asked the Kapi Aga if it would repeat the performance. He replied that it would in an hour's time. "I want to see it," he said.

The Kapi Aga, who was an intelligent man, was not sure whether I had programmed that, since he knew I had set it to go off only four times in twenty four hours. He came out to me where I was standing at the side of the house to hear the organ, and asked if it would perform again in an hour. I told him it would not because I did not think that the Sultan would have stayed so long. But if, when the clock struck, he would like to touch with his finger a little pin that I had previously showed him, it would go at any time. It meant he could keep his promise to the Sultan. When the clock began to strike again the Kapi Aga went and stood by it. As soon as it struck twenty three he touched the pin and it performed as before.

The Sultan said it was excellent. He sat down right in front of the keyboard where you would sit to play it by hand. He asked about the keys that moved without anyone touching them when the organ played. The Kapi Aga said that they enabled the instrument to be played at any time. The Sultan asked if he knew anyone who could play it. He said he did not, except for the man who brought it and he was outside the door.

"Fetch him here," said the Sultan, "and let me see how he does it."

The Kapi Aga opened the door I had gone out of. He came out and took me by the hand and smiled. I asked my interpreter what I was supposed to do and where I was going. He replied that it was the Sultan's pleasure to hear me play the organ. So I went with him.

I went through the door and was astonished by what I saw. I came in to the right of the Sultan about sixteen paces away. He did not turn his head to look at me. He was magnificently regal but it was nothing compared with the retinue that stood behind him, a vision that made me think I was in another world. The Sultan sat still, looking at the Present in front of him, while I stood dazzled by the people behind him, four hundred of them. Two hundred were his principal pages, the youngest sixteen years old, some twenty and some thirty. They were dressed in calf length coats and matching caps of gold lamé, with long pieces of silk around the waist for a belt and knee-length red Cordovan leather boots. Their heads were shaved except for a locks of hair like a squirrel's tail behind the ear. They were clean shaven apart from moustaches. They were all good-looking men and Christian by birth. Another hundred were deaf-mutes and also dressed in rich gold lamé and Cordovan boots. But their caps were of violet velvet with the crown like a leather bottle and five peaked corners on the brims. Some of them had hawks on their fists. The remaining hundred were all dwarves, big bodied men but small. Every dwarf had a scimitar by his side and they were also dressed in gold lamé. I was most amazed by the deaf-mutes for they communicated perfectly with signs everything they had seen the Present perform.

I watched this wonderful spectacle for nearly a quarter of an hour. I heard the Sultan say something to the Kapi Aga who stood next to him. He came up to me, took off my cloak and put it down on the carpet. He told me to go and play the organ. But I refused because the Sultan sat so close to where I had to stand to play that I could only do it by turning my back on him and touching his knee with my breeches, which nobody was allowed to do except the Kapi Aga, on pain of death. So he smiled and let me stand there for a moment. Then the Sultan spoke again and the Kapi Aga cheerfully told me to pluck up courage and pushed me forwards. When I got near the Sultan I bowed my head down to my knees, without my cap falling off, turned my back on him and touched his knee with my breeches. He sat on a rich throne. On his thumb was a diamond half an inch square, at his side a beautiful scimitar, a bow and a quiver of arrows. He sat behind me so he could not see what I was doing. He stood up and the Kapi Aga moved his chair to one side so he could see my hands. As he stood up he could not help pushing me forwards, since he sat so close to me. I thought he was drawing his sword to cut off my head.

I stood there playing until the clock struck. I bowed as low as I could and stepped away with my back towards him. As I was picking up my cloak the Kapi Aga came up and told me to stay there and leave my cloak on the floor. After a little while he told me to go and put the cover on the keyboard. I went near the Sultan again and bowed and shuffled backwards to my cloak. When they saw me doing this they all laughed. I saw the Sultan hold his hand out behind him full of gold, which the Kapi Aga took and gave to me. It was forty-five sequins, more than two hundred pounds. I was taken out the way I came, not a little pleased with my success.

Once outside the Seraglio I hurried to the gate where the ambassador came in. He and his party had been waiting two hours for the Sultan to go to another building to deliver his letters. When I got there I saw the ambassador getting on his horse to leave. He saw me and came up and asked if the Sultan had seen the Present. I told him he had and that I had seen the Sultan, who gave me gold out of his own pocket. He looked very pleased with this. While he was talking to me two smart Turks rode up and asked him to get in position and stay there a while. The ambassador told me to stay with him as he wanted to hear more of my good news.

As soon as everyone was in place a great gate opened in the courtyard and suddenly five hundred men came out on horseback. They had handsome uniforms and excellent horses. Then came five hundred janissaries on foot. Each of them carried a long cane like a beadle's staff and they also had impressive uniforms. The thousand men only crossed the courtyard for show. When they had gone, six splendid Turks on fine horses came to our ambassador and escorted him to the water's edge.

When the ambassador came back to his own house he and the twelve gentlemen went into his chamber and sent for me to tell him what the Sultan did when he saw the Present and how I got to see him. When I told him what had happened they were all very pleased that he had liked it so much. But the ambassador sat quiet for a good while and said nothing until someone asked what he was thinking about, seeing that everything had gone so well. The ambassador said that there was one thing he regretted. It never crossed his mind that I would come into the Sultan's presence and neither did anyone else mention the possibility. If he had had the slightest suspicion he would have spent thirty or forty shillings on clothes for me.

September 31st

I was sent for again to the Seraglio to put right some settings they had changed. The two cadets who looked after the house made me very welcome and asked if I would be happy to remain there for ever. I would not want for anything but have everything my heart desired. I said I had a wife and children waiting for me in England.

They asked me how long I had been married and how many children I had. In fact I had had neither wife nor children and was using it as an excuse. They told me that if I stayed, the Sultan would give me two wives, either two of his concubines or two of the most beautiful virgins I could find for myself in the city or the country.

The same evening, as the ambassador was at supper, I told him about the conversation in the Seraglio and what they had offered me to remain there. He said I should under no circumstances flatly refuse anything but be as agreeable to them as possible and tell them that if the Sultan wished I would be very happy to stay. If I said this they would not try to force me to stay and I would be able to find an opportunity to go when I pleased.

THE HAREM

October 2nd

The ambassador hosted a dinner on board our ship and invited the Venetian ambassador and several Turks.

October 12th

Friday. I was invited to the Seraglio and also on the following Sunday and Monday for no other reason than to see the Sultan's private chambers, his gold and silver, and his thrones. The person who invited me had me sit down on one of them and draw the sword out of its sheath, with which he crowns his kings. When he had shown me many other things that I admired, we crossed a little square courtyard paved with marble. He pointed to a grating in the wall but made signs that he could not go up to it himself. The wall was very thick with a heavy iron grating on both sides. Through them I saw thirty of the Sultan's concubines playing ball in a courtyard. At first I thought they were young men but then I saw their hair hanging down their backs in plaits with tassels of little pearls, and other obvious signs, and I realised they were women and very pretty at that. They wore little gold lamé skull caps. Around their necks were pretty pearl necklaces and jewel pendants and jewel earrings. They had loose coats like a soldier's of red or blue satin tied with a cord of the opposite colour. You could see their thighs through the calf length cotton trousers, snow white and fine as muslin. Some of them wore Cordovan knee boots others had bare legs with a gold ankle bracelet and velvet platform shoes four or five inches high.

I stood so long looking at them that the cadet who was showing me around lost his temper. He looked angry and stamped his foot to make me come away, which I was very reluctant to do as it was a lovely sight. We went back to where we left my interpreter and told him I had seen thirty of the Sultan's concubines. He advised me not to talk about it in case any of the Turks heard about it, for if it got out it would mean death for the man who showed me. The cadet did not dare look at them himself. Although I watched them for so long, they did not see me or look over to the grating. If they had seen me they would all have come over to look at me and been as amazed at how I got there as I was to see them. *(This is probably the first ever recorded glimpse inside the Sultan's harem by a foreigner.)*

STAYING ON

October 12th

The next day our ship the Hector was ready to leave and I took my bed and my chest on board. While I was there a messenger came to the ambassador with an express command forbidding the ship to depart but to remain at the Sultan's pleasure. The ambassador wondered what the reason could be. He thought there might have been some breach of contract or an offence to some great person. Whatever it was the Sultan had to be obeyed. After he had thought long and hard what the reason could be, he went to the messenger and asked why the Sultan had issued this command. The messenger said he did not know but had heard that if the craftsman who set up the Present in the Seraglio could not be persuaded to stay behind, the ship had to remain until he had moved it to a different place. When the ambassador got this much out of him he was more cheerful, for he had been very concerned that it was a much more serious matter. The merchants had contracted in the sum of five hundred pound with the owners of the ship to leave on the following Thursday, wind and weather permitting. After that demurrage was twenty pounds a day.

The ambassador sent someone to the ship to fetch me. When I arrived he was with another messenger who confirmed that the only reason for the command was that I had to stay behind in order to move the organ somewhere else. When the ambassador told me that I had to stay and let the ship go I was very upset. In a fury I told him that all my fears had been realised, which were that in the end he would betray me and hand me over to the Turks to live the life of a slave and never again be among Christians, and other similar words.

The ambassador patiently let me speak my mind. Then he put his hand on my shoulder and said that as he was a Christian himself and thereby hoped for salvation, it was not a plot and the first he heard of it was when the messenger arrived. Finally he said:

"Let the ship go and I promise you five hundred pounds if you are forced to stay a day longer than you wish after you have moved the Present. You may stay here as long as you like or leave as soon as you like and choose your travelling companions. You will have as much silver and gold as you need to travel by sea or land. You will travel ten times more safely and comfortably than if you went with the ship because she is going to Iskenderun and is not on the way home. She will stay there at least a month to take on her cargo. The place is so unhealthy that many of her crew will get sick and die but you will be out of danger."

The ambassador's words were so friendly and genuine that he soon changed my mind. I told him I would trust in God and in him. He said

"Thank you. I will send to the ship for everything you need, for you should go right now to the Seraglio to see where you are to set up the Present, or else they will think you don't intend to come at all."

So I went with my interpreter back to the gates of the Seraglio. I had a warm welcome in the pavilion where the

Present was installed. My old friends the cadets, who were its custodians and had been instructed by the Sultan to persuade me to stay there for good, which they had attempted several times and in different ways, now thought I would indeed stay on and embraced me and covered me with kisses.

I am not certain but I think my interpreter told them that I was not going to to stay on. I went outside and down four or five steps into the courtyard and was putting on my shoes when one of the cadets came up behind me and lifted me up in his arms and carried me back up inside and put me down at the door where all the Sultan's brothers were strangled on the day he became Emperor. My interpreter hurried after me. When the cadet put me down I told my interpreter to ask why he had done that. Seeing that I found it funny he laughed heartily himself and said he had done so to see how I would take it if they forced me to stay. I told my interpreter to tell him that they did not have to find ways of keeping me by force for I would willingly stay to do the Sultan every service I was able.

NARROW ESCAPE

The two cadets took me to see the house where the Present was to be moved. The path through the gardens was very attractive, with many well maintained cypress and fruit trees. After the gardens we came out onto a beautiful lawn where we found some fine-looking Turks riding horses on the east side next to the Seraglio wall. On the seaward side is a lovely little building, called a kiosk or pavilion, which is meant as a banqueting room. I was told that the Sultan met his concubines there twice a week. It has a flat roof covered in lead and a little square tower in the middle of it with a gilded turret. On the seaward side is a pretty balcony from where you can see up and down the Dardanelles and over into Asia. On the other three sides facing the lawn are large porches supported with fine marble pillars and beautiful carpets on the floor. The ceilings are intricately decorated with gilt and paintwork. It is marvellous when you go inside, I cannot properly describe it, but the roof is concave ...

MISSING PAGE IN DALLAM'S MANUSCRIPT

...pipes and laid them out in order on the carpet. I asked my interpreter why they were running away. He said the Sultan and his concubines were coming and we had to leave or lose our heads. They all ran away and left me behind. Before I got out of the house they were across the lawn and out of the gate. I ran as fast as my legs would carry me. Four black men chased after me with their scimitars. If they had caught me they would have hacked me to pieces. At the gate many cadets were praying that I would escape the clutches of those wolves and were overjoyed when I reached safety. I did not stay around but took a boat and went straight away to the ambassador and told him how I had run for my life. As soon as my interpreter came home, the ambassador told him he would hang for leaving me in danger. In the end he spared his life but told him never to come back. He was a Turk but born a Cornishman.

While I was running away I saw something of the spectacle of the Sultan on horseback with his concubines, some riding and some on foot, and some splendid eunuchs in charge of them, and jet black men with great scimitars at their sides in golden scabbards.

October 21st

The ambassador would not let me go to work as it was the Sabbath. I lost out because the Sultan had arranged to come and sit with me and see how I put everything together. When he got to the lawn the cadets ran to meet him and told him that I was not coming to work that day. He went back and did not come again because he thought I had stayed away on purpose.

October 24th

I finished my work.

October 25th

I went to the Seraglio again with the Kapi Aga to show him one or two things about the Present and to make sure I had left nothing undone. The two cadets tried very hard to persuade me to stay.

October 31st

The ambassador went to the Vizier's house with his retinue of Englishmen. The Vizier had arranged to end a dispute with the French ambassador. But when the French ambassador saw us going past his house with more men than he could muster he refused to follow us, which did nothing for his reputation. The two ambassadors were petitioning for the same thing and the Vizier received enormous bribes from the French ambassador. *(Lello had told the Vizier that Henry IV of France had converted to Catholicism and allied with Spain and so was unreliable. This got back to the French ambassador and caused a diplomatic rumpus.)*

LEAVING CONSTANTINOPLE

November 12th

I went to the Adrianople gate, the furthest gate of Constantinople on the Adrianople road. On the plain outside the gate I saw a caravan of the biggest camels I ever saw in my life. We came back to the city to see various monuments, which I would not have missed for anything. I do not have time to write about them now, so will nt list them until I have more leisure. In the morning I put on a pair of new shoes and wore them out before evening. But I overdid it and caught a severe chill. I had a burning fever and my life was in danger.

By the time I had recovered, with the help of God and a good doctor, it so happened that there was a group of people getting ready to leave for England. There would not be a similar opportunity for another two or three years if I stayed behind and they were all happy for me to go with them. The ambassador was most unwilling for me to go because I was very weak and incapable of walking more than a mile a day. But I begged the ambassador to give me leave for I would rather die on the road home than die in Constantinople, as I was convinced I would if I stayed behind.

The ambassador wanted me to take my bed with me and gave orders for it to be taken on board and also, that if we travelled overland, there would be a horse to carry me and another to carry my bed and my clothes.

November 28th

Wednesday. At four o'clock in the afternoon we left the city of Constantinople and Galata on a Turkish ship called a karamursel. It was an unpleasant voyage because of the barbarous captain and crew. The next day we came to the two castles of Sestos and Abydos where some of our group went ashore and bought as good wine as you can find anywhere in the world, but only for their own consumption.

December 1st

After seven miles we came to the ruins of Troy and sailed past Tenedos, leaving it on our left. The wind was too strong for our light ship and we dropped anchor at the island of Lemnos. We were in great danger of losing our anchor.

December 6th

We set sail again with a fair wind but were becalmed by evening.

December 7th

The wind was against us so we dropped anchor by the coast of Roumeli, the mainland of Greece.

December 8th

We set sail with a fair wind and entered the Gulf of Volos.

OVERLAND

December 9th

Sunday. We landed at Volos in Roumeli not far from Thessalonika. Reluctantly we mounted our horses and started our journey overland, crossing into Thessaly. *(What follows is the first account in English of a journey across the mainland of Greece.)*

December 12th

In the evening we came to the town of Lamia. Our horses and mules went back to Volos and we rested for two days. I say rested but I am sure we had no rest at night as our lodgings were so bad and we lived in fear of having our throats cut. Our only comfort was that we had plenty of good wine and good mutton.

We hired fresh horses and mules. There were only eight of us but we had twelve horses. Four of them carried our clothes and my bed and wine and supplies for three days. We were likely to sleep out of doors some nights and in some towns we could not find any provisions. While we were in Lamia we were warned to stay together for some of the Sultan's troops were on their way back from the wars.

December 14th

We left Lamia. Leaving behind six or seven mules we began to climb Mount Parnassus where we had all kinds of bad weather, thunder, lightning, rain and snow. The road was so bad I don't think Christians ever had such a journey. The mountains were immense and steep and rocky and the paths very narrow. If a horse were to stumble or slip, horse and rider would have been in danger of their lives.

In addition we were followed by four rough-looking villains. They were Turks and tried to persuade our interpreter, who was also our guide, to let them cut our throats in the night. He very wisely concealed this from us and passed the time of day with them, not daring to turn them down outright. So they followed us four days over Parnassus. Our guide told us to keep a good look-out, especially on the last night, as they did not mean to follow us any further and he had told them they could do the deed then. After he warned us to keep watch he went over to them them and gave them so much wine, or put something in the wine, that they were ill as well as drunk. They were incapable of doing us any harm, for which we gave heartfelt thanks to Almighty God our chiefest safeguard.

That night we slept in a little village under a massive cliff. Although that part of the world is always cold the women never wear anything on their feet. They are very good-looking but their feet are black and wide.

Our guide and interpreter was an Englishman born in Chorley, Lancashire. His name was Finch. He was totally Turkish by religion but he was our faithful friend.

December 17th

We had winter and summer on the same day. In the morning we walked on ice and snow. Before noon we reached the foot of the mountain and a river so wide and fast and full of stones that we did not dare cross it. Our Turk rode up and down the bank and found two big fellows, who were naked and half wild. He shouted to them and they reluctantly came over. He talked to them and asked one of them to take his horse by the bridle and lead him through the river. He did so with the help of a long staff. Then the other wild man took Mr Paul Pindar's horse and led him over, then Sir Humphrey Conisby and so on. The thick and muddy water was simply snow melt from the mountains where it snows continually. Some time before evening we came to Lepanto or Nafpaktos which is a sizeable port town. The majority of the inhabitants are Jews followed by Turks and then Greeks. It lies close to the sea, rising uphill to a castle with double walls. In several parts of town are very fine fountains with excellent water. Some of them drive mills of a unusual construction in that only a water wheel without cogs or anything else turns the stone. They can grind thirty bushels a day or more. I can give directions how to build one.

They have plenty of very pleasant wines, both white and red. They also grow a lot of currants, oranges and lemons, citrons, pomegranates, dates, almonds and very good oil.

We stayed three nights in the house of a Jew, who is called 'the honest Jew' by the English, as he is well disposed towards them.

It was here that our guide told us all about the brigands. We only once caught a glimpse of them. It was why he never rode with us for very long but was with the Turks discussing their evil plot.

ARCADIA

December 20th

We took a boat and crossed the Gulf of Lepanto to Patras in the Morea. We had high hopes of being well entertained by Mr Jonas Aldridge, an Englishman who was consul there. But he had gone forty miles away to have a Jew hanged. We had to stay at a Greek's house with the same amenities as we had throughout our journey. Although we had room enough we slept in our clothes on the floor. The exception was the Jew's house in Lepanto where there were two beds, English style, but which could not accommodate us all. Mr Conisby would like as not have cut off the head of a Jew who railed against our Saviour if Mr Paul Pindar and the rest of us had not, with great difficulty, stopped him.

Patras is in the Morea which adjoins or is part of Greece. It is a good port but the town is half a mile from the sea on a hillside. A little way above the town is a castle but neither are well fortified. They produce a fair amount of currants and oil and a great deal of corn, which they export to other countries. There are also lots of goats and sheep and other animals. Some of us were sick so we stayed there three days.

December 24th

Christmas Eve. We continued our journey through the Morea. At noon we came to a river we had to cross. We decided to eat there as we always had provisions for three days. We set up in the shade of some alder trees out of the sun, for although it was Christmas Eve it was as hot as England at Whitsun and there were swallows flying around. After dinner we crossed the river and went into a forest where we saw no towns or villages but only the occasional shepherd's hut. At night we came across three poor cottages. It was wild country so four of us slept and four kept watch for we thought it a dangerous place. I was one of the four who took the first watch. Between eleven and twelve o'clock we saw a ball of fire, big as a football, rise out of the east to a great height. It was very bright. Then it went down to the west and the light faded. Mr Conisby was very sorry he had not seen the fireball.

December 25th

Christmas Day. We set off at four o'clock in the morning. We passed countless herds of pigs as well as sheep and goats. We were continually pestered by sheepdogs, which almost dragged us off our horses. We were in the plain of Arcadia. After about an hour we came to a village where we thought we could buy some supplies but got only eight eggs. The weather had been fine the day before but about a mile beyond the town on the plain it bucketed down with rain. The horses stood stock still. It lasted no more than a quarter of an hour and in that time for a mile around us we could not see the ground for water. Suddenly it stopped and the water disappeared, except for a few puddles. Crossing the plain we could see the sea on our right and countless wild swans on the beach. On the left were tall mountains.

At night we came to a castle on a high hill three miles from the sea called Castel Tornese. It has a Turkish garrison and could be held with very few men. The way up to it is so difficult that cannon cannot come anywhere near it.

December 26th

On St Steven's day we intended to cross over to Zakynthos but the wind was too strong.

ZAKYNTHOS AGAIN

January 6th

On St John's day the wind dropped and we carried our provisions and our luggage down to the sea where we hoped to find boats going across. We found a market for pigs and other animals that is held every day in good weather. Zakynthos imports all its food from there. It is only twelve to eighteen miles by sea but we had a lot of difficulty hiring a boat to take us. We paid seven sequins, more than thirty pounds. Here beside the sea we parted with our interpreter who had been our guide from

Constantinople. Although he was a Turk his name was Finch and he was born in Chorley, Lancashire.

We were not allowed to go ashore in Zakynthos because the authorities learned that we had come from Constantinople. They always do this with foreigners coming from Turkey if they do not have a Venetian or Italian health certificate. The Governor and the two Signors of Health locked us up for ten days in the lazaretto which is a prison for travellers. If at the end of ten days anyone is sick when the Signors of Health visit, they have to stay there another ten days.

January 7th

Our merchants, who do business there, managed to get us pratique, or permission to leave. When we arrived we thought we would have to stay longer in prison but they did us the great favour of putting us in a new house beside the sea, where nobody had lived before. The boatmen who had brought us from Castel Tornese were also detained with us and we had to find provisions them for a week. The Signors of Health came to see if any one of us was sick. Mr Paul Pindar asked them to release the boatmen so we would not have the burden of feeding them. They were happy to give the boatmen pratique, or their liberty, if they jumped out of a window into the sea with their clothes on and washed themselves all over. They were very reluctant to do this but Mr Conisby drew his scimitar and swore that if they didn't jump out of the window straight away he would cut their legs off. This induced them to jump out and so we were rid of them.

A lot of other things happened while we were detained but I do not have time to record them.

HOMEWARD BOUND

February 26th

We left Zakynthos after a wait of forty six days for a ship to come in that would take us to Venice or England. The first to come was the Hector in which I came out from England. We thought she would have been back in England by that time. When I saw her I was a little disappointed for I really wanted to go to Venice. But I soon cheered up because I knew we were sure to get a passage home and with men who knew me.

February 27th

We had bad weather and a contrary wind so went back and dropped anchor at Cephalonia. With us was the Edward Bonaventure and the Swallow. In the harbour we found the great Susan of London, three hundred tons, and the Royal Defence of Bristol.

February 28th

The merchant ship Bonaventure came in.

March 1st

A little ship called the Diamond came in. Cephalonia has very good Muscat wine and currants. The harbour is excellent and ships are safe whatever the weather. We set out in a flotilla of eight ships. Twenty miles out to sea the wind turned against us and the weather looked ominous so we went back to the harbour again. In the morning the wind turned and we set sail once more.

March 6th

We passed the Gulf of Venice. A moderate south-westerly gale prevented us from holding our course but at night, as we were going round, the wind turned south-east and held for the next day.

March 9th

We saw Mount Etna, the volcano in Sicily. In the afternoon we sailed by the coast. At first we did not think to drop anchor because the wind was so bad but beating up and down we saw the watch towers light signals to show other watch towers how many enemy ships they saw. If a tower shows as many lights as there are ships, the news goes round the island in a short time. Had we dropped anchor we would not have been afraid of them but they would have been afraid of us. Suspecting that the wind would worsen or else would drop completely, we kept out to sea.

March 9th

The next day we were close enough to the shore to see a great troop of soldiers both cavalry and infantry. Nevertheless we dropped anchor. When the wind turned fair every ship set sail before anchors were weighed. The other seven ships gave chase to a Spanish ship going to Malta with wheat. When she saw so many English ships under sail she thought it better to go back to Sicily than hold her course. As we had been the hindmost of the eight we were now in the lead and took the prize. It was only a small boat laden with wheat. When our sailors finished looting her our captain gave the ship and the wheat to Captain Coke, a man-of-war. We had some very fine white bread and good cheese out of her.

That night a mighty storm came up with a westerly wind. We had gone a hundred and twenty miles past Cape Passero when we finally dropped anchor. The storm lasted forty eight hours in which we could not put up any sail. The prize we had taken was driven ashore.

March 13th

Wednesday. We were driven back a hundred and twenty miles and Cape Passero came back into view. We dropped anchor and met with a large Flemish ship. That night the watch towers made their signals again. The next morning we weighed anchor but were driven further back and that night we returned to the same place. We took it as a punishment for taking the prize.

March 16th

It was very calm and extremely hot. At eight o'clock in the evening we set sail for the wind rose fair from the east into a moderate gale. The next day we were becalmed between Malta and Sicily.

March 19th

Near the coast of Sicily we met an English ship called the John-and-Francis laden with Turks and Jews making for Alexandria.

March 21st

Good Friday. The wind turned fair and brought us to the island of Pantelleria.

March 23rd

Easter Day. The wind was directly against us and drove us back.

March 25th

Tuesday We met the Rebecca of London and the Green Dragon of Bristol.

March 29th

With a fair wind we passed Cap Bon. Forty miles on we passed a little island with a high mountain called Zembra and then Porto Farina on the same day.

SEA CREATURES

April 1st

We crossed the Gulf of Tunis. Our provisions being very low I was invited to dinner with our merchants in the main cabin. We heard the cry of a mermaid hailing our ship. The bosun forbade us to answer or look out. *(This was April Fool's Day.)*

April 2nd

The wind blew fair.

April 3rd

The wind was against us so we dropped anchor at Formentera, where our boats went ashore for fresh water and provisions. It was inhabited only by convicts. Near a watch tower we came across a man without a head, which we supposed had been cut off by Turks. The island is very near the Spanish island of Ibiza. Our ship rode a little way off the town and castle, which is very well fortified.

April 6th

Sunday. In the morning, as we were weighing anchor, a boat came from the town with presents for our merchants of two goats, oranges, lemons, leeks, onions, green beans, lettuce and other vegetables.

April 7th

We sailed past Las Calderones and Alicante, which is four hundred miles from the mouth of the Straits. There we met two Flemish ships from Wallonia.

April 9th

We passed Cape Palos and the following night Cape de Gata. In the morning we were becalmed before Alhama, a beautiful Spanish town not much inferior to London, so it is said. We were becalmed all that day and the following night.

During the day we saw a lot of whale spawn, which they use to make spermaceti. It floated on the water where the whale left it. It looked red on the water but when we took some of it up in a bucket it was white and greasy. *(A common misapprehension that spermaceti*

comes from whale semen, hence the name. It is in fact a
wax found in a whale's head. What did they find? Algae?)

On the same day a moderate gale blew up. A big fish
called a shark, which is extremely long, followed alongside
our ship with his eyes out of the water looking for prey. If
a man in the water had come within a length of him, he
would not get away. Our master gunner got his harpoon
ready. Whenever the clever fish saw him about to throw it
at him it dropped behind and came up on the other side.
This happened two or three times. At last the gunner
struck him hard behind the head but the skin was so hard
that the iron bent and would not go in. All we could see
was a little white spot where it hit. The fish did not
appear to have felt it but then left us.

April 11th

The wind was dead against us. As we were tacking to
make some use of it we came very close to the shore near
Castell de Ferro in Spain. We expected them to shoot at
us but they did not. Then, less than a league from the
shore, we had no wind at all and so it continued for the
rest of the day. Our flotilla was scattered a league from
each other so that if Spanish galleys had come out they
could have taken us one after another.

It was wonderful to see the porpoises running in great
schools and to hear the noise they made.

April 13th

We met a ship out of Yarmouth.

April 15th

We made for Gibraltar where we met three English ships and one Flemish, which brought our flotilla up to fourteen. But the wind was so contrary that we could not get into the narrow channel at the mouth of the straits but lay becalmed between Marbella and Malaga

April 16th

We were becalmed. The next morning we saw two whales that were so enormous we thought they were galleys or frigates. It was an extremely hot day.

THE LAST ADVENTURE

April 17th

At ten o'clock the wind came up fair from the north-east so about eleven o'clock at night we entered the narrow channel, which is fifteen miles long. As the sun rose we passed Cape Spartel, forty miles the other side of the mouth of the straits. We could see twenty-one ships.

The same day the fastest ship of our flotilla, the Rebecca, left us with the intention of bringing the first news to England of our safe return home.

April 20th

Sunday. Very early a lookout in the maintop saw a sail coming straight towards us. When we made out her hull we saw it was the Rebecca, the same ship that left us two days before to take the news of our home-coming to

England. Two Spanish galleons were in pursuit, although not as fast as her. The captain of the Rebecca thought they were galleons coming from the Indies and loaded with valuable cargo, but he was much mistaken. They were men-of-war lying in wait for our ship, as they afterwards confessed. As they came near we also thought they were coming from the Indies. One of them was a thousand two hundred tons and the other eight hundred. Our captain was very unwilling to do battle but our crew was keen. So after prayers the gunners made ready the cannon, the screens were put out, every man took his place and everything made ready. We had the wind of them. The Hector came alongside the big galleon and another English ship, the Great Susan, came alongside the other, waiting to see who would fire first. The rest of the flotilla was ahead of us and more than a league away...

MISSING PAGES RELATE THE BATTLE, RESULTING IN A VICTORY FOR THE ENGLISH.

...have leave to go ashore and take post horses to London. At last he gave me and three others permission, on condition that we took the Spanish captain with us and delivered him safely to the merchants, which we promised to do. We went ashore at Dover. Our trumpets blew in front of us all the way into town where we celebrated all we could, so happy we were to be on English soil again. After dinner a French ambassador came into town accompanied by various knights and gentlemen of Kent. So at two o'clock we took post horses to

Canterbury and from there to Rochester, where we spent the night. The next day we came into London.

The End

4 WHAT HAPPENED NEXT?

Thomas Dallam was born probably in 1575 near Warrington in Lancashire so he was about twenty four years old when he went to Constantinople. When he came back his reputation was made and he flourished as an organ builder. In 1605 he built an organ for King's College Cambridge and continued to service it until 1641. He looked after the organ in Magdalen College Oxford. In 1613 he supplied an organ to Worcester Cathedral and in 1617 to Holyrood House, Edinburgh. He married and had a son, Robert, in 1602, and some time later a second son Ralph. They joined him in the family business and became respected organ builders in their own right. We do not know when Thomas died but it was after 1641.

None of Dallam's organs survive, at least which we can attribute. Several were destroyed and the pipes melted down by Puritans in the 1650's, including those in King's College and Worcester Cathedral. We do not know what happened to Michael Watson the carpenter and John Harvey the engineer. Rowland Buckett the painter had a successful career. His work is still to be seen on an organ which Dallam erected at Hatfield House, the country seat of the Cecil family. He also worked for Edward Alleyn at Dulwich College. He died in 1639.

Henry Lello finally managed to present his credentials and remained ambassador until he returned to London in 1606. English trading concessions were granted in 1601. He was succeeded by Thomas Glover, a long term resident of Constantinople. He was recalled in 1610 after diplomatic misjudgements.

Paul Pindar was appointed consul at Aleppo in 1606. In 1611 he followed Thomas Glover as ambassador in Constantinople. He returned to London in 1620 and continued to build his fortune in the City of London. He died a rich man in 1650. The oak facade of his house in Bishopsgate is in the Victoria and Albert Museum.

The choleric Humphrey Conisby became a treasurer to Elizabeth I. The Kapi Aga, the Great White Eunuch, was executed in the reign of Sultan Mehmed's son, Ahmed. Queen Elizabeth I died in 1603. She was succeeded by James I.

Sultan Mehmed III also died in 1603. He was succeeded by his thirteen year old son Ahmed I, whose mother, a Greek, was his co-regent until he was fifteen. A devout Muslim, Ahmed commissioned the mosque that bears his name, known as the Blue Mosque. He also demonstrated his religious fervour by an aversion to the depiction of living things. He destroyed Dallam's organ, by all accounts in person with a battleaxe, and ordered the remains to be burned. So the Present lasted about five years.

5 MORE ABOUT THE ORGAN

An article on page 380 of The Illustrated London News of the 20th October, 1860 reproduces a drawing and specification of what is probably the organ clock which Dallam took to Constantinople. The article does not mention where the original documents were found. The organ was commissioned by the Governor of the Levant Company from Randolph Bull, a member of the Goldsmith's Company and clockmaker to the Queen.

The base was carved oak. Above it was a gilded and painted panel-arch. On each side of it were two smaller panel-arches, with sixteen fluted and carved pillars. After the second frieze, which was of carved oak, there was a keyboard. Above was a dial marked with twenty four hours. The pipes on either side were carved and gilded oak. After another carved oak frieze there were four towers, one in each corner, each tower supported by sixteen pillars, and the whole surmounted by a vase and crescent. In the centre of the platform on which the towers stood was a figure of Queen Elizabeth, adorned with forty-five precious stones including diamonds, emeralds, and rubies. Encircling her Majesty were eight other figures

Above the next frieze were the Royal arms embossed, painted, and gilded, and on each side a trumpeter. Above the next was a mechanical head to announce the hour. On top of everything was a cock with a pyramid on each side and finished with a gilded crescent.

Inside the base were three mechanically operated bellows that could power the instrument for up to six hours, an organ barrel and three sets of pipes, an open principal unison recorder, octavo principal, and a flute along with a tremolo, plus a drum and a nightingale. The entire contraption was to play automatically four or five songs without anyone touching the keys for six hours without interruption.

In the middle part of the instrument behind the dial and pipes, were nine separate mechanisms. The first was a clock showing the progress of the sun and the moon, the moon's phases and the position of the planets. The second was a man in armour, standing on one of the towers, who struck a bell every quarter of an hour. The third was another man in armour on another tower who struck the twelve daytime hours. The fourth was a cock who fluttered his wings and crowed on the hour. The fifth was a chime of bells that could be set to play at any hour. The sixth was for all these figures to pay homage to Her Majesty and for her to acknowledge each one by raising her sceptre. The seventh was for two trumpeters to lift their trumpets to their mouths and sound them as often as required. The eighth was for the head to open its mouth and roll its eyes on the hour. The ninth was for an angel to turn an hour glass on the hour. Delivery was to be ten months and the instrument guaranteed for seven years. The price was £550.

Dallam's organ sounds very similar, although a holly bush full of blackbirds and thrushes replaced the crowing cock.

This is how the organ was described by the Kizlar Aga in his account of its destruction by Sultan Ahmed some time after 1603. "It was about five feet in width and depth, and more than the height of a man. On it were pictures and diverse figures, some of them stringed instruments, some flutes, some layers of six-stringed lutes, some drums, some drummers. It showed various kinds of stringed instrument apart from these. At the turn of every hour, from each picture and figure came some sort of movement and some kind of admonitory gesture. The instruments in their hands or mouths gave out wondrous notes and marvellous sounds and voices, such that the mind wondered how to describe them, and men of intelligence were too perplexed to define them." *(Translated by Professor Geoffrey Lewis and quoted in 'The Rise of Oriental Travel' by Gerald M Maclean.)*

6 ACKNOWLEDGMENTS

The British Library bought Thomas Dallam's original manuscript in 1848. It was transcribed by J. Theodore Bent and published in 1893 by the Hakluyt Society in *Early Voyages and Travels in the Levant.* You can download various digital versions from http:// www.archive.org/details/earlyvoyagestrav00dallrich

Scholars have pointed out that J. Theodore Bent ignored additions by Dallam in the margins of his text and a few of his transcriptions and notes are evidently flawed. However, his is the only printed version available and the one I have used.

In 1956 Putnam published *An Organ for the Sultan* by Stanley Mayes. This is a readable and well-researched account, good for the background, history and other contemporary sources. His treatment of the actual journey is novelistic and the diary embroidered. I have found no digital version and copies are rare outside libraries.

In 2004 Palgrave Macmillan published the enlightening *The Rise of Oriental Travel. English Visitors to the Ottoman Empire, 1580-1720* by Gerald M. Maclean. He discusses four travellers, including Dallam, in the context of Anglo-Ottoman relations, English attitudes to Islam and developing ideas of what it was to be English. From this book I have taken the Kizlar Aga's description of the organ. Print and digital editions are available from online bookshops.

Specifications for the organ are in the Illustrated London News 20th October, 1860. See http://gale.cengage.co.uk/ product-highlights/ history/ illustrated-london-news.aspx for how to access the Illustrated London News.

Finally, many thanks to Diane Latty, Chris Wootton, Nuala, Alex and Damian Mole for invaluable help with editing and proofing.

John Mole has published three comic novels – *Sail or Return, The Monogamist* and *Thanks, Eddie!* In 1992 He published *Mind Your Manners*, a guide to the business cultures of the new Europe.

In 2004 he published a travel memoirs, *It's All Greek To Me!* followed by *I Was A Potato Oligarch* in 2008. His latest novel is *The Hero of Negropont,* a traveler's tale set in Ottoman Greece

He lives in London and Greece

www.johnmole.com